FACE TO FACE

FACE TO FACE

WITH JOHN FREEMAN

INTERVIEWS FROM THE BBC TV SERIES
INTRODUCED BY JOAN BAKEWELL

BBC BOOKS

Published by BBC Books
a division of BBC Enterprises Limited
80 Wood Lane, London W12 0TT

First published 1989

© John Freeman and the contributors 1989

ISBN 0 563 20805 8

Set in 10/12 Bembo by Ace Filmsetting, Frome
Printed and bound in Great Britain by
Mackays of Chatham, PLC
Jacket printed by Belmont Press, Northampton

Contents

INTRODUCTION

by Joan Bakewell

Thirty years ago, the BBC launched a television series that was to prove a landmark in broadcasting. It was called *Face to Face*; its interviewer was John Freeman and it brought a whole range of outstanding and famous people to the screen.

The viewing public had seen nothing like it before: interviews that gently but insistently probed the lives and personalities of people of outstanding achievement.

The programmes were nearly always transmitted live from the Lime Grove studios in London. And I can recall what a remarkable stir they made. There was no BBC 2 in those days; Channel Four wasn't even a glimmer on the horizon; and videos, with all their options, nasty and otherwise, hadn't been invented. So it seemed as though the entire nation settled down to watch *Face to Face* – and then talked about it.

The interviews soon became compulsive viewing, instant classics. So too did the opening titles: the lilting theme from a Berlioz overture matched with the artist Felix Topolski's line drawings of that week's guest. They gradually dissolved into the actual face of the celebrity: novelist Evelyn Waugh . . . poet Edith Sitwell . . . philosopher Bertrand Russell . . . sculptor Henry Moore.

The first *Face to Face* interview went out in February 1959, watched by an audience of 4.5 million. Over the next three years, an impressive array of individuals agreed to be interviewed. They ranged from international statesmen like King Hussein of Jordan to great artists like Augustus John, and to popular names of the day such as pop star Adam Faith and playwright John Osborne.

A total of thirty-five interviews were recorded and – an interesting sign of the times – only two were with women. Altogether, they are a unique record of some of the towering figures of the century.

Face to Face was hugely popular; it was also one of the most controversial programmes on the air. The two often go together. It tried to unmask for the first time on screen the private faces of public figures, to peel off their protective layers and expose what was hidden underneath. Viewers nowadays are used to robust, even impertinent interviewing and guests have learned to dodge and parry, to deflect or simply stonewall questions they don't like. But these were pioneering days and *Face to Face* just wasn't like that. Guests seemed genuinely willing to collaborate in a search for the truth about themselves.

Sometimes it was more painful than they anticipated. This was partly due to the setting. The interviewer, John Freeman, was rarely seen. Only the back of his head featured. The lighting was harsh and unflattering and the cameras broke with convention and came closer than ever before.

Some interviews were described as torture by television. Critics complained the guests looked as if they were being brainwashed, interrogated, fried alive by the lights; unfortunate subjects made to look like gargoyles. *The Times* proclaimed that the programme's attraction was in seeing how the next man stood up to the rack. In particular, the interview with TV quiz personality Gilbert Harding left a lasting impression and became a talking-point among the nation. John Freeman was acting as psychoanalyst, some said, by asking such personal and probing questions. The interview with Tony Hancock attracted similar criticisms.

It was moments like these which made John Freeman into a celebrity himself. Elegant, courteous, already well known as a presenter of *Panorama*, it was *Face to Face* which really brought him fame. His departure brought an end to the series in 1962. He went on to edit the *New Statesman*, became British ambassador to the United States and, later, head of London Weekend Television. Aged seventy-three, he now lives in California, where he lectures part-time.

Eleven of his famous programmes were chosen for the repeat series shown in the autumn of 1988 and are printed here, with the exception of the interview with Tony Hancock which his family did not want published. Also included are three *Face to Face* interviews – with Henry Moore, Stirling Moss and Victor Gollancz – which appeared only in the original series. To launch the repeat series, John Freeman agreed to be interviewed by a man who has taken over his role of persuading celebrities to reveal the private person beneath the public face. Dr Anthony Clare, himself a psychiatrist and presenter of Radio 4's series *In the Psychiatrist's Chair*, came face to face with John Freeman, in California.

JOHN FREEMAN

Anthony Clare interviews
JOHN FREEMAN

CLARE Professor Freeman, you have had a most eminent career ever since you graduated from Oxford just before the Second World War. You had a brief period in advertising before distinguished service in that war, you were demobbed as a major, with an MBE. You were then an MP in the postwar Labour government before you left politics, to some extent at any rate, and went into journalism. You served as ambassador to the United States, having been a high commissioner in India. You were chairman of London Weekend Television, chairman of ITN, you were awarded the gold medal of the Royal Television Society. You are here now as a visiting professor, at the University of California in Davis, yet many people remember you almost entirely for the series of interviews known as *Face to Face*. Does that surprise you?

FREEMAN I think . . . I feel gratified that anybody should remember me for anything but certainly *Face to Face* attracted a lot of publicity at the time so it doesn't altogether surprise me.

CLARE But looking back at it all those years ago, it's very nearly thirty years, does it surprise you that the interest has been maintained?

FREEMAN It does. I wonder whether it *has* been maintained. You will have to put this to the test and see. I was surprised that the BBC decided to run these programes again. I hope I may say I think they were quite good in their day, but most of the people who took part are now dead, and after all television and interviewing have come a very long way over the last thirty years.

CLARE So if I told you that there is still interest, that would surprise you.

FREEMAN Yes, it does surprise me.

CLARE Now, you say that television and interviewing have come a long way and you, at the time, presumably thought that this would be a pioneering approach which would, in a sense, become routine.

FREEMAN I'm not sure whether I really thought that at the time. I thought I was earning my living and this was an interesting way to do it. I think, looking back on it, that there was an element of pioneering about it, but it wasn't my doing, it was the producer of the programmes, Hugh Burnett, who was the pioneer and what was striking about the programmes, as I recall them, was simply the camera work. The subjecting of a notable public person to interrogation and subjecting him simultaneously to the very, very close scrutiny of the cameras. People who are going to watch these programmes again will see that the camera hardly ever moves out of close-up on the face, every bead of sweat, every flicker of the eyelid is visible, and that was a dimension which, to the best of my knowledge, hadn't existed in television before and the credit for that is Hugh Burnett's.

CLARE Now, what about the fact that it was never done again?

FREEMAN I could never understand that. We reached the time when I decided I didn't want to go on doing it, and I have no doubt that the series could have been maintained and that there were other interviewers who would have been at least as capable as I who could have continued it, and I have to say that I urged this on the BBC, but they decided to kill it. And when I think that this was at the time when interviewers like – to take one as an example – Robert Kee, whom I regard as my superior in almost every respect, was at the height of his career, a man like that could easily have done it. I don't know whether he was ever asked to but it's a great pity, I think, that the series didn't go on.

CLARE How did it come about?

FREEMAN It came about, as far as I know, because Hugh Burnett had done some comparable work in radio, that is to say, very intensive and close interviewing of public figures, and thought this should be transferred to television, and he had the idea that I've already referred to, using the camera almost as a second interrogator, and the idea I think was a good one. He and I had worked together in television, in the past, and he suggested that I should be his journeyman to do the interviewing, which pleased me, and that's how it started.

CLARE Whose idea was it that you would not be visible on camera?

FREEMAN Well, I don't remember. It was probably Hugh's but it may have been mine. It was an idea, at any rate, that I strongly applauded and I guess he started it. The whole point of the programme was that the subject who was being interviewed should have the whole of the screen the whole of the time and that to show the interviewer's face would be a total distraction.

CLARE I'll come back to that because, of course, it was one of the features of the series that people remember and, again, it is one of the features that has not since been copied. But let me put to you something about why I think it might not have been copied.

When you had completed *Face to Face*, which was in 1962, you had done thirty-five interviews, which again is something I think people don't realise, there were a large number of interviews. About twenty years later I came to do a series of interviews on BBC Radio, which were called *In Depth*, and I immediately came across your shadow.

FREEMAN Mm!

CLARE There was much discussion – this is 1982 – about in-depth interviewing, and they recalled *Face to Face*, they being people in broadcasting, with a certain degree of mixed feelings.

Now, what I'm putting to you is that in one sense it was a remarkably pioneering approach but in another sense it actually froze everything and it did this because two things were combined in the public mind, which don't necessarily go together. The first was what you set out to do, which was to take the mask off public figures and show what lay beneath, a perfectly reasonable thing to do. The second was the technique, the camera, as you say, showing the beads of sweat, the head, the face; the interviewer relatively unemotional, emotionless, dispassionate, uninvolved, not there to comfort if somebody wept or to intervene, but very much the camera really, the camera interviewing; the lights, of course. And the impression, at any rate, which I suppose might have owed something to the 1950s at the time and the preoccupation with, if you like, brainwashing techniques, the impression that there was something unholy about the process. And that was paired: the actual activity that you were engaged in, very reasonable; the technology, rather frightening.

FREEMAN I don't know what to say to that. The fact is the programme made a tremendous impact visually, I would like to think it made an impact in its verbal content as well, but it made a tremendous impact visually and it has to be seen as a whole. I don't think that the people who took part in it felt that it was an unholy alliance, and you were speaking a minute ago about pioneering. What was new about it was simply that, for the first time, the interviewer and the camera and the lights and the studio environment were all integrated into a single concentration on the individual who was being interviewed.

Now – dispassionate. I was a journalist, it seemed to me my job to be dispassionate and, in any case, I thought one got more out of people one was interviewing if one was dispassionate.

CLARE The fact remains it wasn't done again.

11

FREEMAN Right. Well, I've told you I don't know why that was. It may be people didn't approve of it.

CLARE What did you make – because, clearly, in terms of your responses at the time, you were surprised – what did you make of the tendency of critics to describe it as, indeed, searching and revealing, so there was again, as I say, the positive side, but also as inquisitorial, cold, intrusive, like being interviewed by a computer. Did that surprise you?

FREEMAN No, not particularly. Incidentally, not all critics took that view but some of them did, and I respect their opinions. You know, one puts oneself up, in the business of entertainment and enlightenment, and one has to be judged by other people as they find one. It didn't surprise me particularly.

I suppose I would defend my techniques – if they can be thus described! – by saying that it seemed to me that that's how one got most out of the people one was interviewing. It wasn't intended hostilely or harshly or cruelly and, indeed, some of them I became great friends with afterwards.

CLARE Such as Tony Hancock.*

FREEMAN Such as Tony Hancock.

CLARE Can I just take that interview because it was the subject of much discussion and it was one of the few, I think, that provoked you into print. What I wanted to know was, when he was coping with your questioning, was there at any stage a feeling, on your part, that he wasn't able to cope or that he was in a corner?

FREEMAN You're asking two different questions. Yes, of course, he was in a corner once or twice, I hope that you, as an interviewer, would not regard it as a fault if you occasionally put a subject into a corner. But that he couldn't cope, no. Tony coped perfectly well. He was, as I learnt to know later, a somewhat inarticulate man off the stage anyway, and he coped in his own way, but he was a man of great sensitivity, a lot of intelligence, and I was interested, in that interview, you know, in the old *Pagliacci* theme, the sorrow behind the mask of laughter and so on, of which he was a prime example, and I thought that the public would be interested in seeing a little of the torment which goes into the making of a great comic. And he was one of the greatest comics.

The press fulminated about the harsh way in which I'd treated him; Tony and I became firm friends for the rest of his life.

*Broadcast on 7 February 1960. Repeated on 9 October 1988. Not included in this selection at the request of Hancock's family.

CLARE Sticking with that interview, though I don't want to necessarily talk about individual interviews in great detail, I was struck by a preoccupation which perhaps reflected the fifties and that was how much he earned, which certainly stung the critics. You were rather interested in it.

FREEMAN If so I've forgotten exactly why, but it's not a question which is unasked even nowadays. I think that with public figures, particularly in the world of entertainment, people are interested in knowing how much they earn. I'd forgotten completely asking him about that but if I did I'm not surprised and I don't think I need to apologise for it.

CLARE Let me ask you about this business of interviewing in depth. It's been compared, and I think you've written yourself using this kind of imagery, that it's a bit like detaching a mask, a surgical exploration to some extent. The person is participating freely so there's no question of compulsion. None the less, and it's said to me so I'm putting it to you, not as an accusation but because I'm interested in your view on this, it's said that there's something partial.

If you start to uncover, the psychotherapist at least has the potential and the time to cope with the wounds if there are any and heal them to some extent. The problem with television or radio interviewing is that we have but the time to uncover, and that you can then leave people rather raw and the viewer or the listener rather pained. What would you say to that?

FREEMAN Well, I don't think I can answer that question as far as the viewer is concerned. As far as the subject of the interview is concerned, well, it's quite true, journalists have less time and less skill than psychiatrists, I entirely agree with that, they're working with much more rough and ready tools.

But it does seem to me that public figures, whether they're in politics or in show business or otherwise volunteering to be public figures, must expect that the public will want to know a little bit what they're really like, and the point of Face to Face, or the point of Face to Face as far as I saw it, was that I wanted to ask the sort of questions which I thought an intelligent person, given the chance to ask, might wish to ask that particular person. So, if it was a politician, I perhaps would try to find discrepancies or illogical attitudes, if it was a comic, I might try to explore the sadness which lay behind the comedy, if it was an actress, I might be interested in how much she earned or what her private life was like, but it wasn't a kind of prurient inquisitiveness, at least I didn't see it like that, it was a desire to help people to see their idols free of the sort of public relations imagery which surrounds most public people most of the time. So that they could look at whomever it may be, Lord Reith, Sir Robert Boothby,* or whomever, and say, That's a nice guy, or, I don't like him, and have some reason for making the judgement. And that seems to be the function of a journalist, which is very, very different from your function as a psychiatrist.

CLARE Oh yes, and I wasn't for a minute suggesting one was superior to the other because the hazards I have are precisely that if I were to distress someone, on television or radio, I wouldn't have the justification that the journalist might have, that that's the rules of the game; I have also got other professional responsibilities.

But, in your case, you were a very hardened professional journalist, I mean you were doing a lot of work on *Panorama* at the same time, and I wondered about you crossing the boundary in the opposite direction, you coming from journalism, if you like, to psychological exploration. I go in the opposite direction, and I'm conscious of this. It's a sensitive area. The judgements involved are actually quite delicate sometimes.

FREEMAN Well, I understand what you're saying. I didn't see this as psychological exploration –

CLARE You didn't.

FREEMAN – I think you're magnifying it or using grandiloquent language about it. I didn't see it as psychological exploration. There was a guy, sitting in that chair, who was well known to the public for this, that, or the other reason. Let's see what he's really like: is he a nice chap or is he a nasty chap, has he got common sense or not, does he really believe what he's saying. These seemed to me to be questions that the public not only are entitled to ask but do ask, and if an interviewer can help them to get the answer, so much the better.

CLARE None the less, the ones that are remembered – I know to your irritation and I share it because you did so many others and they're very formidable and several of them are going to be shown in this series – but none the less you are remembered for two or three where I think the psychological aspect was at its strongest: Hancock, Gilbert Harding, Evelyn Waugh; and if I took Harding's interview, the question that really turned everything was the question when you asked him had he ever actually been present at a dying patient's bedside. Now that's a rather psychological question. It cues in, and it did, to a very interesting aspect of this rather complicated and not very clear man.

*Broadcast on 27 May 1959. Not included in this selection.

FREEMAN Well –

CLARE In other words, not the sort of question I'd expect John Freeman, *Panorama* interviewer, to ask.

FREEMAN Well, it was a question which I realised immediately afterwards shouldn't have been asked and I always made it quite clear that I regretted asking that question because, quite unknown to me, it did touch on a very sensitive point. This maybe I should have known about but didn't know about at all. I thought, as I remember, that Harding was speaking rather loosely and freely of these emotions and I simply wanted to find out whether what he was saying was grounded in any sort of experience. I subsequently found out that not only was it grounded in experience but in a very poignant and recent experience which he'd had, and had I known that I would never have asked him the question.

CLARE You wouldn't.

FREEMAN No, certainly not.

CLARE So the question, in a sense, which very largely one interview in particular is remembered for, was something of a mistake.

FREEMAN It was, yes. It was simply no doubt my fault that I was not aware of the background enough to realise that that particular question went beyond the bounds of civilised conversation.

CLARE Even though it did what you, in a sense, said the series was setting out to do –

FREEMAN Well, yes.

CLARE – to show the man behind the public mask. The mask was an irascible –

FREEMAN Well, that's right –

CLARE – bad-tempered man and here he was soft and emotional –

FREEMAN Yes, well, this is true and I think that at the end of the day, Harding, although, poor old boy, he wept, I don't think he suffered. I think people did see him as an altogether more human character than they had before, and that was to the good.
    Nevertheless, you know: who will rid me of this turbulent priest. If I want to shut someone up, if I stick a knife in his heart it's one way of doing it, but it's not the recommended way.

CLARE Yes. You talk about revealing. Were you, yourself, surprised ever in an interview?

FREEMAN Oh, constantly.

CLARE Can you recall that kind of experience?

FREEMAN Well, it's difficult to be specific because it really happened the whole time.

CLARE Well, did Reith surprise you?

FREEMAN In many ways he did. Actually I was going to give you, on the tip of my tongue, a different example from that; one that surprised me very much was the racing driver, Stirling Moss. Now, it had appeared to me, from reading the cuttings and finding out what I readily could find out about him, that this was a playboy with a talent for driving fast cars, and he was no doubt justly world champion motor racer and so on, but I thought that he was only a playboy.

I was astonished to find out what an intensely serious professional he is, and I remember asking him at some point in that interview, where fear came into this, and he dismissed the concept of fear completely saying it wasn't a matter of fear, it was a matter of calculation, had you got the calculation right or not. If you'd got the calculation right there was nothing to be afraid of. This was a man of cold, precise, clinical engineering judgement, and that surprised me very much indeed.

CLARE Did it appeal to you?

FREEMAN It did appeal to me, yes, it did appeal to me because the notion that a man could live so close to the edge of death and danger, and trust entirely to his own judgement to keep on the right side of that line, I found very stimulating.

CLARE The reason I asked that is that I sometimes felt, watching the interviews, that you're a man, yourself, who greatly prizes reason and logic and perhaps is not terribly – and wasn't, with the interviews – terribly happy when emotions bubbled up.

FREEMAN That's a judgement which you may well make and it may be correct. I don't think I can answer it.

CLARE In talking about the Moss interview, is that one that you would say was a particularly satisfying one?

FREEMAN Yes, for what my opinion is worth, I think that is the best of the whole lot, in a technical sense, that's to say I don't say that a huge public is still interested in what happened to Stirling Moss, but I think that as explaining or giving an insight into a public character, in a courteous and reasonable and gentle, but I hope insistent and persistent manner, I think that interview was the best of them all.

And it is incidentally almost the only interview I can ever recall doing on *Face to Face* or anywhere else, from which I came away reasonably satisfied!

CLARE I was going to ask you that. Yes, whether you'd agree with me that this is a process, an activity which leaves one always feeling a sense of dissatisfaction. It's very hard to come away from an interview without remembering all the things one wished one had done and indeed a lot of things one wished one hadn't done. You would agree.

FREEMAN Absolutely, absolutely. I mean, I think it's partly because we're fallible humans and no doubt a great deal more stupid than we like to pretend! And, secondly, I think you have to remember that, you know as well as I do or better, the constraints of time are paramount and one forgets things, it's as simple as that, one forgets things sometimes that one ought not to forget.

CLARE The constraints on you were really quite enormous. I'm not sure everybody realises these were programmes that were filmed live, they were done live.

FREEMAN Almost all of them, yes.

CLARE Almost all of them, that's right, there were one or two . . . Carl Jung was done in –

FREEMAN In Zurich, yes.

CLARE – in Zurich. They were done within the timespan, that's to say you recorded or you filmed exactly the same length of time as they went out, they went out live of course, so you didn't see many of them.

FREEMAN I've seen hardly any of them myself, to tell you the truth. The only ones I've ever seen are the handful that occasionally the BBC shows on ceremonial occasions along with the trumpet players and so on, they occasionally put on three minutes of *Face to Face* and I've sometimes seen those. But I think I saw certainly hardly any of them, if any of them, at the time they went out.

CLARE Because once done they were done.

FREEMAN Well, most of them went out live, that's three-quarters of the answer, and the rest of it I think is what you just said, I was a working journalist, I was earning my living as best I could, I'd done a job and I was doing something else the next day.

CLARE Was there a profoundly unsatisfactory interview, one that you do look back to with horror, you wouldn't like to see re-emerge?

FREEMAN Well, I don't know that there's one that I look back on with horror, I think that would be an overstatement, but there was one that disappointed me profoundly, which perhaps is almost the same thing, and that's the interview with Otto Klemperer.*

Now, Klemperer was a man whom I admired enormously as a musician, and indeed I knew him a little and liked him as a man. He was a formidable and terrifying figure, as anybody in any of his orchestras will no doubt confirm. But he was a very entertaining and intelligent and nice man, and I thought that really I would be doing some public service by getting him on to this programme and he agreed to come.

And, when we started, I suppose it was nerves on his part, but his English simply wasn't up to it, and I sat there for twenty-seven and a half minutes, knowing that I was sitting on a gold-mine and that it only required a little bit more skill to get it all out. And I couldn't do it, and he became more and more garbled, and things that I knew he could talk about and would probably like to talk about, came out all sort of muddled and confused, and it was a nightmare for me.

Judging from the way the interview was received, the public didn't see it as quite as bad as I did but it was a terrible disappointment because it's one of those that I would have liked to be remembered as among the best and instead of which it was among the worst.

CLARE Did you, during the recording of these thirty-five interviews, did you learn anything about yourself that you hadn't known before?

FREEMAN Well, I don't think so. I don't know whether that sounds modest or immodest but I think the truth is not very much because, after all, this was one series of programmes, and it attracted a lot of public attention, but I was in the business, I was interviewing as a journalist in both print and television and radio, every day of the year, and it sounds a rather downbeat and awful thing to say but I suppose the truth is that this series was a good deal less important to me than it was to many of the people who criticised it.

CLARE Yes. I mean, how curious about people would you say you are?

FREEMAN Oh, I think I'm quite curious about people. Incidentally, one of the golden rules, I would have said, for interviewing people is that you must want to know the answer. It's no good asking questions which are written down on a clipboard, and you ask the question and then your mind wanders and you begin to think of something else while he's answering it. You must want to know the answer, you must

---

*Broadcast on 8 January 1961. Not included in this selection.

be inquisitive enough to want to know, and then the thing gets a momentum of its own and keeps going and, of course, the interviewer is then in a position to change direction if he sees advantage in doing so. So I did want to know the answers.

CLARE That must have been one of the problems at the time, constraints. You must have found yourself wanting to follow something but also knowing that there were other things you wanted to cover that might lead to something.

FREEMAN Yes, well, this is true and I think I probably quite enjoy living with that kind of television, and one of the areas in which one can easily make mistakes, and where I did make mistakes, was in not judging correctly what particular line would be fruitful and what wouldn't. You know, sometimes one got it right, sometimes one got it wrong.

CLARE One of the interviews that I was very struck by, in relation to this, because you had so many avenues you could follow, was with Carl Jung. And particularly that moment where you ask him does he still believe in God and he says, It's not so much a matter of I believe in God; I know. And then you rapidly changed gear and went into something else. And I wondered whether that was one of those moments where Jung would want to have followed it and yet there were a lot of other things you were left with, his relations with Freud and so on.

FREEMAN Well, I realised afterwards, because that's one that's been played so often that I have seen it, I realised afterwards that I should have followed that up. I didn't follow it up, not so much because I wanted to change the subject, as because I thought I understood in the context exactly what he was saying, but I realised afterwards that viewers hadn't and I should have followed it up.

CLARE About that interview, how reluctant was Jung to be interviewed? I ask that because I think despite the fact that the visual media were around a long time, and Jung was one of the giants, whether one likes it or not, I don't recall any interview with him on television other than yours.

FREEMAN Yes, I'm not aware of another one, there may be, I don't know. I think that he wasn't in the event all that reluctant and he told me – now I'm not going to take any responsibility for this, I don't know whether it's true – but he told me the reason that he'd accepted so readily was that he'd had a recent dream, in which he had seen himself standing in a market-place with a great crowd of people round him, and he was addressing them and teaching them, a

Messianic sort of conception if you like, but he was teaching them, and, as a result of that dream, shortly afterwards the invitation from the BBC came along and he decided to accept it. Now, you take that or leave it, that's what he told me.

CLARE And that's how you did it.

FREEMAN And that's how I did it.

CLARE You stopped after thirty-five. They were spread over about three years. Why did you stop?

FREEMAN Well, there were two reasons. I mean, other things interested me more, and I also found that it was extremely tiresome and unrewarding to be treated as a sort of celebrity merely because I was performing in a television programme, and I'd been innocent enough not to realise that a successful television programme led to that kind of distortion of one's life and I didn't care for it and so I stopped.

CLARE Isn't it really curious that, despite the fact that you were not on camera, you were not seen, the same thing happened to you as if you had been. Indeed, you are remembered, in some ways, more than many of the thirty-five whose heads were seen so brilliantly on television for half an hour each evening back in the 1950s and 1960s; you are remembered and yet you were not seen.

FREEMAN Well, in that programme I wasn't seen. I was seen pretty often in others, but still, it's true, I can't explain that, that's the public for you, but what I will tell you is that when nowadays – and it happens, I have to tell you, even today, thirty years later – I am still from time to time recognised, when I go about in England, it is always the voice and not the face which leads to the identification. Now, when I think of my silly voice, I'm astonished, but there it is. People hear me, let us say in a pub or something like that, hear me talking and come up and identify me from that. So it shows that the face is not the only, is not the all-important part of identification.

CLARE It's the voice as much.

FREEMAN It's the voice as well.

CLARE Looking back, do you feel that the experience with *Face to Face* justifies that approach? In other words, that there should be something like it as a feature of contemporary television, that it has a role to play and that its lack is that, is a lack, and not just a sensible decision by television not to deal with something which should be left to other things, to other areas.

FREEMAN You know – I'm sorry, I don't want to sound rude to you – but that's the sort of portentous question which I don't think I want to answer on those terms.

I mean, what I think is that one of the functions television can perform for the public, if it's properly used, is removing some of the layers of public relations glitz which tend to cover public figures and it ought to be used for that purpose amongst others. *Face to Face* was one way of doing it.

I was a journalist, I was asked to do the programme, I did it to make a buck or two and earn my living, I enjoyed it, I hope it was well done while it was done. I was sorry it was discontinued at the time, because it was a going concern. I don't think I've got any views about whether it should be re-created now.

CLARE John Freeman, thank you very much indeed.

FREEMAN Thank you.

LORD BIRKETT

INTRODUCTION

For his very first programme in the *Face to Face* series, back in February 1959, John Freeman was understandably nervous. Not only was the programme going out live, but his first guest was himself an eminent cross-examiner and judge – Lord Birkett.

It's hard for us to imagine in the 1980s the extent to which, in those days, murder trials and other dramatic court cases occupied the public's attention. As a cross-examiner in the 1920s and 1930s Norman Birkett had become well known for his appearances in dozens of famous, often grisly trials – trials that sound like the titles of detective novels: 'The Green Bicycle Case', 'The Blazing Car Case' and 'The Brighton Trunk Murder'. Usually appearing for the defence, Birkett was popularly known as 'The Man Who Always Gets Them Off', and in 1935 he was even among the top twenty favourite personalities of the day in a newspaper poll.

After a distinguished career at the Bar, Birkett was elected to the Bench in 1941, and as a judge he took part in a landmark in legal and international history – the Nuremberg trials of Nazi leaders and war criminals. He helped to devise the Nuremberg principles, which laid down for all time how war crimes and crimes against humanity were to be defined.

He was created a baron in 1958, becoming Lord Birkett of Ulverston. He died four years later.

This *Face to Face* was John Freeman's first, but Lord Birkett had already participated in, and enjoyed, its predecessor: a series of personal interviews for BBC Radio in the Far East made by the same producer, Hugh Burnett. This television version introduced what was then the radical new technique of close camera work and the virtual invisibility of the interviewer. It aroused considerable comment: some viewers complained about the back of John Freeman's head; others found his questions a little too personal. Nearly all, however, were enthralled by the programme.

After it was transmitted, the television personality Gilbert Harding – later a famous *Face to Face* guest himself – burst into the studio to offer his congratulations, and viewers jammed the switchboards with expressions of praise for Birkett's modesty and integrity, his command of the English language and his gentle manner.

INTERVIEW

FREEMAN Lord Birkett, you are known to the world, I suppose as one of the three or four greatest criminal lawyers of this century, and perhaps one of the three or four greatest cross-examiners of all time. Now, I want you to tell me, face to face, what manner of man you really are. First, then, about the law. Do your murder trials stand out in your own memory as great dramatic highlights?

BIRKETT One or two of them do, I think. There's a danger of rather exaggerating their importance. The number of murder trials, or indeed criminal trials, that one takes part in are a very small part of one's work. But Dr Ruxton, or the Rouse trial down at Northampton, both struck me as being very dramatic indeed.

FREEMAN Do you happen to remember how many successful murder defences you undertook in your career at the Bar?

BIRKETT If it doesn't sound immodest, it's easier to remember those in which I failed!

FREEMAN Well, how many did you fail in?

BIRKETT Well, three, I think.

FREEMAN Did you always believe in the innocence of your clients when you defended them?

BIRKETT To be quite, quite frank, no. I think I just ought to say that whatever your belief is, you're not allowed to state it in the court. You're allowed to speak as an advocate, but you mustn't give your own opinion.

FREEMAN Did you personally ever have any qualms about defending someone on a murder charge, whom you believed to be guilty?

BIRKETT None. You see, the view I took of the advocate's duty, and I think it's the right one, is this. He's there to present one side only, and he must do it to the very best of his ability, and what he thinks really is irrelevant.

FREEMAN Would you think that it was your duty as counsel to use every possible trick within the law to get a man acquitted?

BIRKETT I would be against tricks of all kinds; but if you would alter the question to saying, 'Do you regard it as your duty to do everything within your *power*, within the *rules*, to get him acquitted', I would say yes.

FREEMAN Yes. And that would include, perhaps, bamboozling a jury?

BIRKETT Well, shall I say, *persuading* a jury. I wouldn't bamboozle them. What you do is to try and persuade them to your point of view.

FREEMAN Have you ever got a man or a woman acquitted on a murder charge whom you believed in your heart to be guilty?

BIRKETT Yes.

FREEMAN Any regrets about that?

BIRKETT None.

FREEMAN Have you ever defended a person on a murder charge whom you *knew* to be guilty?

BIRKETT No. Indeed, you're not allowed to. You may think that he is guilty, and of course it's really quite impossible for any man of sense to have a brief to defend some man, and read all the facts, without coming to some conclusion in his mind, but that's quite irrelevant. He's not the judge.

FREEMAN Did you ever refuse a brief because of moral certainty that the person who offered it to you was guilty?

BIRKETT Never.

FREEMAN Have you ever felt sure that someone convicted on a capital charge was innocent?

BIRKETT Never.

FREEMAN So that you know of no case where a man has gone to the gallows wrongly?

BIRKETT Never.

FREEMAN Now, I believe I'm right in saying – correct me if I'm wrong – that you never defended in a blackmail case in your career. Is that pure coincidence or – ?

BIRKETT Pure coincidence. Yes, pure coincidence.

FREEMAN You would never refuse a brief because you disliked the kind of offence which was alleged?

BIRKETT Oh, no, indeed. Otherwise, one would refuse half the cases.

But the criminal side of one's practice is comparatively small compared with the civil.

FREEMAN Nevertheless, you would surely agree that a great deal of your public reputation was based on your exploits in the criminal courts? Now, what was it that particularly attracted you, because it's true, isn't it, that many lawyers affect to look down a little on criminal practice?

BIRKETT Well, I found a very great fascination in winning twelve people to my point of view. There is a very great attraction and fascination in the exercise of persuasive speech, and I daresay, if one began to analyse it, that was one of the factors.

FREEMAN It's always said of you that your great asset in persuasive speech was the appearance of sincerity. Do you agree with that?

BIRKETT Well, if so, it wasn't, so to speak, a piece of acting. It's quite impossible to persuade a jury by talking nonsense, and the thing that you say must at least have the appearance of sound sense; otherwise it's no good. And when you're presenting that to the jury, you must certainly give the impression that you are sincere.

FREEMAN Even in those cases where your own private belief was that your client was guilty?

BIRKETT Yes, well, let me take just an illustration: Dr Ruxton, a man who was charged with the murder of his wife and his nursemaid. Well, nobody could read, as I read, all the facts the prosecution were going to prove, without feeling, well, this is a very, very difficult case. But it didn't make me any the less eager to do everything that I could for Dr Ruxton.

FREEMAN Is it true that when Ruxton eventually went to jail after his conviction he made a will in which he left a small bequest to you?

BIRKETT He did.

FREEMAN Did you ever get the bequest?

BIRKETT I asked that I shouldn't have it.

FREEMAN I see. Do you know what it was?

BIRKETT It was a set of fish knives.

FREEMAN You know the practice which has grown up recently of great newspapers paying for the defence of criminals in return for their confessions? Do you approve of that?

BIRKETT Well, in a sense, yes. Providing counsel is left entirely free to conduct the case as he ought to do. I never knew of a case in which I was concerned where it was done, but I believe in one or two famous cases it was done.

FREEMAN Was it not done in the case of Dr Ruxton?

BIRKETT I don't think so.

FREEMAN A confession was published, wasn't it, after his execution?

BIRKETT Was it?

FREEMAN In a newspaper. It was indeed.

BIRKETT It was in Rouse's case, but I don't recall it in Dr Ruxton's. Was it in Ruxton's case?

FREEMAN I understand it was, and I –

BIRKETT Yes, well, I don't think so. My memory isn't quite good enough to say positively, but I don't think so.

FREEMAN At any rate, you had no knowledge of it?

BIRKETT I had no knowledge of it, no.

FREEMAN Now, going right back to your early days, what was it that first attracted you into the law?

BIRKETT Well, it's very difficult to say. I knew nothing about the law when I decided to go to the Bar, and I think the reason was that it offered the best opportunity for using such facility or gift as I had for public speech.

FREEMAN At what age were you when you decided that?

BIRKETT Twenty-six.

FREEMAN I see. And what was your family background?

BIRKETT Well, my father had a drapery business in a little town in the north of England and it was his dearest ambition that I should follow him in that business, and as I cared for my father very much I was very anxious to do what he wished, and for some years was in the business with him; but then I began to yearn for rather wider things, and then I went to Cambridge, and ultimately, as I say, went to the Bar. But I was thirty years of age when I was called to the Bar.

FREEMAN And how did you keep yourself in the time you were reading for the Bar?

BIRKETT I became a private secretary.

FREEMAN What sort of schooling did you have?

BIRKETT Well, I went to the grammar school at Barrow in Furness, and then into my father's business, and then there was an interregnum, and then I went to the university, to Emmanuel College in Cambridge.

FREEMAN Did you ever regret not having been to a public school?

BIRKETT Yes. I'm not sure that it was a wise regret, but I'd like to have made a century for Harrow at Lord's or something of that kind, but on reflection I'm not at all sure that there weren't very many compensations; by the time I went to Cambridge and took part in the debates at the Union I was a fairly practised speaker.

FREEMAN Did you send your son to a public school?

BIRKETT Yes, he went to Stowe.

FREEMAN What sort of upbringing did you have in childhood? I mean, were your family puritanical and stern?

BIRKETT Well, my father and mother, they were Wesleyan Methodists, and I suppose one would say very, very devoted people, and I shall always be grateful for my home life and for the chapel life to which they led me. My knowledge of the Authorised Version and the hymns of Wesley and Watts are certainly some of my very greatest possessions and I shall never cease to be grateful for the training that I had in religious things.

FREEMAN Do you still hold these beliefs yourself?

BIRKETT No. You know, as one grows older one rather grows out of certain ideas, and although I have my own very strong views about the conduct of life and the qualities which are necessary, the great doctrinal things rather perplex me and trouble me. I sometimes would like to say that I called myself a Christian-agnostic, but I don't know whether that term is permissible.

FREEMAN Well, it is to me, but I'm not sure whether it would be to many Christians! Now, getting back to the story of your life, if you were thirty when you were called to the Bar, that I think was in 1913? You've had this terribly busy life – you were an MP for a time, you've been one of the leading counsel at the Bar – would you choose such a busy life if you had your time over again?

BIRKETT Yes, I think so, I think so. My life at the Bar certainly was the happiest period of my life, though every moment of one's day, and almost night, was spent in that work.

FREEMAN Well, exactly. But then what about your family life? Did you, for instance, have enough time to supervise the upbringing of your children?

BIRKETT No, I wouldn't say that I did, myself. I was earning a lot of money and we had good nurses, and household staff, and things of that kind, but I'm bound to say that I didn't do very much in the way of personal supervision.

FREEMAN I think people are always very much interested in the fantastic figures of the earnings which great counsel sometimes make. Will you give some sort of approximation of what perhaps was your best year, your highest point in your career at the Bar?

BIRKETT Well, I can honestly say I never knew how much anybody at the Bar ever made, but I think, from my own experience of the matter, very probably Wilfred Green and John Simon both were in the £50 000 mark.

FREEMAN I was, of course, asking you about Norman Birkett.

BIRKETT I know, but one is a bit shy about giving figures. I earned many thousands – perhaps it would be enough for me to say that when I became a judge, at £5000 a year, it was a terrible financial sacrifice.

FREEMAN Would your old clerk be very inaccurate – he's gone on record somewhere saying that your earnings were about £30 000 a year for many years. Would that be untrue?

BIRKETT Well, it wouldn't be untrue. That would be an average figure, sometimes below it, sometimes above it.

FREEMAN During the course of your busiest practice at the Bar, how many poor people's defences did you undertake?

BIRKETT Well, I always as a matter of principle took on so many a year – very many of the murder cases about which you spoke were done under the poor person's rules, because I always felt it as a kind of duty. The profession had been very good to me, and I thought, Well, I can make some slight return, and I did.

FREEMAN Was that a matter of two or three a year or more?

BIRKETT Rather more, I should think, probably half a dozen, nine or ten, I don't know.

FREEMAN Yes. Now, you did eventually become a judge in I think 1941. Had you ever turned down the opportunity before?

BIRKETT Yes. Because I loved the Bar so much. I think, you know, the life of a judge is a bit remote and a little lonely. You're necessarily withdrawn from the ordinary life of the Bar.

FREEMAN And the remark you've just made means that you did in fact pine for the Bar when you were on the Bench?

BIRKETT Well, pine is a strong word, but shall I say I had slight yearnings that way.

FREEMAN Because it was dull, or because it was isolated, or – ?

BIRKETT Well, to be quite, quite honest, sometimes when I listened to cases being conducted, I felt how much I would like to be down there doing it.

FREEMAN In other words, you missed the chance of appealing to the twelve men that you were talking about earlier.

BIRKETT That's right. That's right, yes.

FREEMAN Do you remember when you gave your first death sentence?

BIRKETT Yes, quite well. I'd always rather dreaded it, but, when the actual moment came, I did it without the slightest trace of emotion.

FREEMAN What sort of case was it?

BIRKETT It was a case during the war, where a young sailor had betrayed the position of a convoy to the Germans, and the Germans attacked and sank the convoy, and the charge was under the Treachery Act, I think, or something of that kind. At any rate, when the moment came for me to sentence him to death, I did it without any emotion at all.

FREEMAN Do you yourself now believe in capital punishment?

BIRKETT Well, I think the Homicide Act of 1957 has really rather solved that problem. I have long thought that capital punishment was on the way out. I'm not sure that the Act of 1957 doesn't raise equally difficult problems, but I think that where you have an element of deterrence, if such there be, there may still be something to be said for capital punishment in certain isolated cases. For example, it's a capital offence for a man to shoot a policeman, and if that deters people I don't see very much harm in retaining that.

FREEMAN You, at any rate, never felt any personal qualms about sentencing a man to death?

BIRKETT No.

FREEMAN Never any doubt that you were doing it justly?

BIRKETT No. You see, it's a very curious thing when you sit in the seat of justice how impartial you become. I won't say you become inhuman. That would be quite wrong. You must keep your human sympathies and your human faculties all alert, but I think you do get a detached, dispassionate outlook upon things which permits you to do your duty. I think so.

FREEMAN Well now, in the world outside this country, I suppose that you're perhaps best known as being one of the judges at the Nuremberg war crimes trial. What did you make of men like Goering and Hess and the rest of them?

BIRKETT Well, of course, I saw them for twelve months, every day, in every possible situation. Goering simply dominated the court. He was a man of very great personality and when he came to give evidence in the witness box he did very well indeed.

FREEMAN Did you at any time have the feeling that you'd got on terms with any of the accused? You warmed a little to Goering, did you?

BIRKETT No, I never did to Goering, largely because I knew his history, and I knew the kind of man he was. The kind of man for whom I felt a little sympathy was a man like Speer, who was only brought in by Hitler towards the end, and was involved in all this, not in creating aggressive war or anything of that kind, but because he took part in the Sauckel policy, of bringing all these people from the other satellite countries.

FREEMAN Did this extraordinary polyglot team of judges, and barristers, and barristers' clerks, and everything else that was assembled at Nuremberg in fact manage to work together?

BIRKETT Ultimately, yes. There was a little difficulty at first with regard to the Russian judges. I sat next to General Nikitchenko throughout the hearings and we became the greatest possible friends, and when we left Nuremberg he promised to keep in touch with me. I've never heard from him since, though I've enquired. But at first the Russian judges were very recalcitrant; if a proposal was raised by one of the German counsel in favour of the defence they were against it, without any argument at all, and one had to try and persuade them to come to one's point of view. It was very, very difficult. But ultimately we worked together.

FREEMAN Now did any of the accused at Nuremberg take the trial seriously – that is to say, did they behave as if they thought there was any possibility of their being acquitted?

BIRKETT Yes, I think so. I think Schacht did. And he was, of course, acquitted. I think a good many of the other people thought, Well, this is merely the victors trying the vanquished.

FREEMAN Well, wasn't it?

BIRKETT Well, it was in truth, but I don't see how that was to be avoided, but the only question I think that can really be asked about Nuremberg is: Was it a fair trial? and I think it was.

FREEMAN Looking back on it, do you think that justice was in the end served by staging a trial without really the existence of a law?

BIRKETT That's commonly stated, which is quite wrong. The charter of 1945 which governed all the activities of the tribunal, certainly set down the law as it existed. It was not a creation of law, it was international law as it existed.

FREEMAN Well, now, could we just look into that for one moment, because none of the soldiers were allowed to plead that they were ordered to do what they did by their superior officers.

BIRKETT Well, but there was nothing new about that. You see, after the First World War, the Leipzig Court, a German court, *they* wouldn't allow the defence of superior orders. And in the charter of 1945 it was expressly stated that superior orders shall not be a defence, but it may be a mitigation. Well, that's always been the law. It's quite true that in our manual of military law there was a mistake, which was amended in 1944, but the true position is that the soldier is bound to obey orders that are not manifestly unlawful. But if he does take part in unlawful activities that really can be no defence.

FREEMAN Well, I hope soldiers will feel comfortable in this dilemma.

BIRKETT Well, I know there's been trouble about this. You see, Field-Marshal Keitel and General Jodl were both convicted and both hanged, but if you examine the Nuremberg records you will find that they weren't just merely acting under superior orders. Take the murder of fifty airmen – the *murder* of fifty airmen! – because that's what it was, they were taken out and shot. And Keitel was very largely responsible for it as indeed Goering was. Is anybody going to say that they could say, Well, you mustn't blame me, because Hitler told me to do it?

FREEMAN At Nuremberg did you play any part in the actual judgment itself?

BIRKETT Yes. Yes. I think I can say that I was present at every sitting, and indeed prepared a good deal of the original judgment for the consideration of the court.

FREEMAN It has been said that you were to some very considerable extent responsible for drafting that judgment. Is that true or not?

BIRKETT Yes, it was true in this sense, that I did the writing of it, and composed it, for the most part, but of course it was always subject to the review of all the judges assembled. I used to write a chapter and submit it to them.

FREEMAN We've been talking about your highlights, your successes and so on. Which is the episode or the period of your life of which you feel *least* proud?

BIRKETT Well, the proper answer I suppose would be 'the whole of it' – that it could have been so much better in so many ways. The real disappointment in my life was that, being a Liberal, the Liberal Party, when I was ready to take part in elections, was on the decline, and therefore I could never be a law officer of the Crown, because you must be in parliament and your party must be in power.

FREEMAN We've got to the time when I must put the last question to you, and it is of course often said, and experience rather bears this out, that politics and the Bar *don't* mix awfully well together in most cases. Now, why is that? Is there some quality which is needed for politics, which the lawyer doesn't have?

BIRKETT Well, you see, in the law, the barrister, the advocate, has all the preparatory work done for him by the solicitor, and he's merely got to get it up and have it firmly in his mind, but in politics he must be rather more original, and I think that's one of the very great difficulties.

FREEMAN And this, therefore, is your lost ambition?

BIRKETT Well, in a sense. At the time I was in the House of Commons I was far too busy to attend. I never got down there until about five o'clock in the evening, and then I had to get up all the briefs for next day; it was that kind of life, and I think that the very busy man really cannot combine the two.

FREEMAN Thank you very much, Lord Birkett.

BIRKETT Thank *you*, indeed.

BERTRAND RUSSELL

INTRODUCTION

In March 1959 John Freeman's guest on *Face to Face* was the out-standing mathematician and philosopher Bertrand Russell – then within two months of his eighty-seventh birthday. But far from being a frail old gentleman, he appeared before the camera as spry, mischievous and articulate as the public had ever known him throughout his long career as a campaigner in various causes at odds with the establishment.

But it was from the establishment he came – grandson of two lords, one of them Lord John Russell, the Liberal Prime Minister. He went to Cambridge in 1890, where he wrote the *Principles of Mathematics* – and later his great work *Principia Mathematica*. His academic work as one of the greatest philosophers of his day con-tinued at Cambridge until the First World War when his vigorous campaigning as a pacifist got him expelled from Trinity. But he continued as a writer, his *History of Western Philosophy*, published in 1945, gaining him a more popular acceptance and lasting financial security.

Russell, a late Victorian, was an early crusader for free love, in revolt against the humbug and hypocrisy of much of Edwardian life – a freedom exemplified unashamedly in his own private life.

After teaching in America he returned to Britain in triumph after the Second World War, was given the Order of Merit in 1949 and won the Nobel Prize for Literature in 1950.

From the fifties onwards his main concern was the threat of nuclear annihilation: he was the first president of the Campaign for Nuclear Disarmament at the time of the *Face to Face* interview, and two years later, still battling against authority, he was arrested at an anti-nuclear sit-in in Parliament Square and sentenced to seven days in jail. He was eighty-nine years old.

His *Face to Face* interview reveals the qualities that sustained his reputation for decades: lucidity of mind, transparent honesty and an endearing sense of fun.

INTERVIEW

ANNOUNCER Tonight we present the second programme in the series *Face to Face*.

RUSSELL *By the death of the third Earl Russell, or Bertrand Russell as he preferred to call himself, at the age of ninety, a link with a very distant past is severed. His grandfather, Lord John Russell, the Victorian Prime Minister, visited Napoleon in Elba. His maternal grandmother was a friend of the Young Pretender's widow. In his youth he did work of importance in mathematical logic but his eccentric attitude during the First World War revealed a lack of balanced judgement which increasingly infected his later writings.*

Perhaps this is attributable, at least in part, to the fact that he did not enjoy the advantages of a public school education but was taught at home by tutors until the age of eighteen, when he entered Trinity College, Cambridge.

In the Second World War he took no public part, having escaped to a neutral country just before its outbreak. In private conversation he was wont to say that homicidal lunatics were well employed in killing each other but that sensible men would keep out of their way while they were doing it. Fortunately, this outlook, which is reminiscent of Bentham, has become rare in this age which recognises that heroism has a value independent of its utility. True, much of what was once the civilised world lies in ruins, but no right-thinking person can admit that those who died for the right in the great struggle have died in vain.

His life, for all its waywardness, had a certain anachronistic consistency, reminiscent of that of the aristocratic rebels of the early nineteenth century. His principles were curious; but such as they were, they governed his actions. In private life he showed none of the acerbity which marred his writing, but was a genial conversationalist, not devoid of human sympathy. He had many friends but had survived almost all of them. Nevertheless, to those who remained, he appeared in extreme old age full of enjoyment, no doubt owing in large measure to his invariable health, for politically during his last years he was as isolated as Milton after the Restoration. He was the last survivor of a dead epoch.

That I wrote in 1937, before the Second World War began, as a prophecy of what I thought *The Times* would say about me when I died. I observe that the date I attributed to my death is 1962, which is coming ominously near.

FREEMAN Well, let us examine this obituary which was written in jest and see how true it really is. To start with, let's go back to the distant past. What is your very earliest memory, Lord Russell?

RUSSELL My earliest at all vivid memories are of arriving at the house of my grandparents (Pembroke Lodge in Richmond Park) after the death of my father, who died when I was three.

FREEMAN How did you come to be in the care of your grandparents? Your mother had also died?

RUSSELL Yes – she also. She died when I was two. My grandfather was already an invalid. He could only get about in a bath chair. He died when I was six. My grandmother survived for a long time, till after I was married, but she lived in semi-retirement. We saw a lot of distinguished people and especially literary people.

FREEMAN Your grandfather had been a politician in his day, as your father?

RUSSELL Yes. My grandfather was twice Prime Minister; my father was in Parliament for a very brief period.

FREEMAN But he held the radical views which we've always associated with the Russell family?

RUSSELL Yes. He held them a good deal more extremely than my grandfather did.

FREEMAN And did your grandmother share these views?

RUSSELL Yes, in a great many ways she did. In some ways not at all. My father lost his seat in Parliament in 1868 for advocating birth control and on that sort of subject my grandmother would not have agreed with him at all; but on purely political issues, yes.

FREEMAN Did you meet the great and famous who used to come to visit? Who especially impressed you at that age?

RUSSELL Well, I think Mr Gladstone especially impressed me. He had an eye that could quell anybody. People who didn't know him can't quite understand his political importance. It depended on his hawk's eye. My most painful recollection of him is when I was seventeen and very, very shy, and he came to stay with my people and I was the only male in the family and after the ladies had retired after dinner I was left tête-à-tête with Mr Gladstone; and he didn't do anything to alleviate my shyness. He made only one remark. He said: 'This is very good port they've given me but why have they given it me in a claret glass?' And I didn't know the answer.

FREEMAN What about your other grandparents, the Stanley family?

Were they very different in their way of life?

RUSSELL Oh, yes. The Stanleys were worldly. My grandfather Stanley (whom I don't remember because he died before I was born) wouldn't allow his daughters to read Thackeray because Thackeray was so true to life, and he took pains that as many as possible of them should marry into the peerage.

FREEMAN I was going to ask you – was either family snobbish about either money or social class?

RUSSELL Well, the Stanleys were, yes. My father's family, no.

FREEMAN Who was your special favourite and confidant of all these elderly relations who surrounded you?

RUSSELL Oh, well, all through my childhood it was my grandmother Russell. In later times when I grew up, well, I don't think any of them were particularly important to me.

FREEMAN Were you always a sceptic from small childhood or did you believe in the conventions?

RUSSELL Oh, I wasn't a sceptic when I was very young, no. I was very deeply religious and lost my conventional beliefs slowly and painfully – very slowly.

FREEMAN Tell me, did you say your prayers when you were a child?

RUSSELL Oh yes.

FREEMAN When did you cease doing that?

RUSSELL Oh, I suppose when I was about twelve or thirteen.

FREEMAN Were you made to say them before that?

RUSSELL Well, yes. I was made to at first but I went on after I'd stopped being made to.

FREEMAN Yes. Will you tell me what experience it was that gave you your first intuition about scepticism when you were a child.

RUSSELL Well, I suppose you might say the time when I tried to catch an angel. They told me when I was an infant that angels watched round my bed while I slept and I'd seen pictures of angels and I thought I should very much like to see one. But I supposed that the moment I opened my eyes they fled away. So I thought, Well, the next time I wake up I won't open my eyes and they won't know. And I did so and I made a grab, thinking I should catch an angel. But I didn't.

FREEMAN Do you think now that you had a happy childhood?

RUSSELL More or less. It was very solitary. I had one brother who was seven years older than me and I had very little to do with him and otherwise I didn't have very much to do with other children. But it wasn't unhappy, no.

FREEMAN Did your loneliness give you any feeling of insecurity?

RUSSELL Well, I was frightfully shy so I suppose one must think so.

FREEMAN Looking back now, with all your learning that you've acquired since, would you say that some feeling of insecurity was one of the spurs to intellectual action?

RUSSELL I don't quite know. I think it's a possible spur. I think there are others of a different sort; I mean, I think pure ambition will sometimes do it.

FREEMAN Yes. Of course, nowadays in the post-Freud world, I think we are better at freeing children from a sense of guilt. Now, were you obsessed at a tender age with a sense of guilt or sin?

RUSSELL Oh yes. They asked me one day what was my favourite hymn and I chose *Weary of Earth and Laden with my Sin*.

FREEMAN And at what age was that?

RUSSELL Six years old.

FREEMAN Do you think now, looking back, that there's any really unfortunate legacy that you carried out of your childhood?

RUSSELL Yes, I do. I mean, the sort of family attitude, certainly on matters of sex, was morbid, morbidly puritanical.

FREEMAN Did you then, in fact, have a feeling of guilt about sex?

RUSSELL Well . . . I don't know. I don't think I had much occasion to, no.

FREEMAN Well now, let's turn to your schooling. You told us in your obituary that you did not go to a public school. Why was that?

RUSSELL Because my grandmother didn't approve of public schools. She was very unconventional in her outlook. She thought they were conventional institutions.

FREEMAN Would you have liked a more conventional education?

RUSSELL No – not at the time, not at all. No, I shouldn't. I was quite satisfied and I think, looking back, I'm still satisfied because I learnt a great deal more than I should have done at any school – a great deal more.

FREEMAN Did you send any of your own children to an ordinary public school?

RUSSELL Yes. My youngest son went to Eton.

FREEMAN And was that successful?

RUSSELL Yes, quite successful.

FREEMAN Tell me now a little about the school that you and your wife ran together between the wars. Why did you start that school in the first place?

RUSSELL Oh well, because I couldn't at that time find a progressive school that I liked. Later I sent my children to Dartington, which I thought very well of, but it wasn't established properly at that time and I couldn't find a school that I liked. We did try a school of our own but it was a failure. Running a school is an administrative enterprise and I have no administrative skill. We had to charge fees. They didn't nearly cover the expense. I lost many thousands of pounds.

FREEMAN Well now, let's turn to your schooling. What sort of learning at that age? Did you, for instance, study the classics?

RUSSELL Well, to a certain degree. I was never fond of the classics. I mean, mathematics was what I liked. My first lesson in mathematics I had from my brother, who started me on Euclid, and I thought it the most lovely stuff I'd ever seen in my life. I didn't know there was anything so nice in the world. But I remember that it was a disappointment because he said: 'Now, we start with axioms.' And I said: 'What are they?' And he said: 'Oh, they're things you've got to admit although we can't prove them.' So I said: 'Why should I admit them if you can't prove them?' And he said: 'Well, if you won't, we can't go on'; and I wanted to see how it went on, so I admitted them pro tem.

FREEMAN Now, what was it that first provided you with the incentive to become a mathematician?

RUSSELL I liked it. Well, for a number of reasons. In the first place, the sheer pleasure, which is the sort that people get from music or from poetry. It just delighted me. And then, apart from that, I thought that mathematics was the key to understanding the universe and I found all sorts of everyday things explained by means of mathematics.

FREEMAN Do you feel that you have succeeded in proving any of the great propositions to which you have devoted your life?

RUSSELL Oh no. No. They are not the sort that you can prove.

FREEMAN Have you found on the whole in your own life that the pursuit of either mathematics or philosophy has given you some sort of substitute for religious emotion?

RUSSELL Yes, it certainly did. Until I was about forty, I should think, I got the sort of satisfaction that Plato says you can get out of mathematics. It was an eternal world, it was a timeless world; it was a world where there was a possibility of a certain kind of perfection.

FREEMAN What episode in your life led you to turn again from philosophy to some extent into social work and politics?

RUSSELL Oh, the first war. The first war made me think that it just won't do to live in an ivory tower. This world is too bad and we must notice it.

FREEMAN Were you a moral pacifist or was it merely that the war seemed to you to have been inexpedient and unnecessary?

RUSSELL I thought, as a politician, and I still think, that it would have been very much better for the world if Britain had remained neutral and the Germans had won a quick victory. We should not have had either the Nazis or the communists if that had happened, because they were both products of the First World War. The war would have been brief. There would have been nothing like so much destruction. I still think that that is valid. That is speaking as a politician. Speaking as a human being, I used to have occasion to go to Waterloo, and there I would see troop trains going off, filled with young men who were almost sure to be slaughtered; and I couldn't bear it. It was too horrible.

FREEMAN How much, in fact, did you actively campaign against it?

RUSSELL Oh, as much as I could. I went all over the place, making speeches, and I did everything I could to help the conscientious objectors. I wrote about it everywhere I could. I did everything I could think of to do.

FREEMAN Did you have a sort of public notoriety as an unpopular figure or were you regarded as just a crank?

RUSSELL I wasn't actually pelted with rotten eggs but I had an almost worse experience. I was at a meeting of pacifists at the Celtic Brotherhood Church and it was stormed by a mixture of colonial troops and drunken viragos. The drunken viragos came in bearing boards full of rusty nails, with which they clamped everybody on the head, and the colonial soldiers looked on and applauded them and the police looked on and did nothing and women had all their clothes torn off their backs, were badly mauled and so forth and so on. The viragos with rusty nails were just about to attack me, and I didn't quite know what one did about this, when somebody went up to the police and said: 'Look, you really ought to stop these women, you know, he's a distinguished writer.' 'Oh?' said the police. 'Yes. He's a well-known philosopher.' 'Oh?' said the police. 'He's the brother of an earl!' – and the police rushed and saved me.

FREEMAN Was this the time that you went to prison?

RUSSELL No, that was earlier.

FREEMAN Well, what exactly did you go to prison for?

RUSSELL For writing an article. I was convicted on the ground that this article was 'intended and likely to cause bad relations between England and the United States', because I pointed out how United States troops were used as strike-breakers and it was thought I oughtn't to have done that.

FREEMAN Did you plead guilty to the charge?

RUSSELL Oh no. I said that it's nonsense if you really think that the United States is going to alter its policy because of an obscure article in a little sheet that nobody reads.

FREEMAN Were you tried by a jury or by a magistrate?

RUSSELL By a magistrate.

FREEMAN In London?

RUSSELL In London and he said this was the most despicable crime.

FREEMAN And what did he sentence you to?

RUSSELL He sentenced me to six months. Originally it was six months as an ordinary criminal and then on appeal it was altered to six months in the first division.

FREEMAN Which meant more lenient treatment?

RUSSELL Oh, very much. It's a profound difference.

FREEMAN Now, I have heard it said that at that stage your family were able to pull strings which gave you treatment quite different even from that of normal first division prisoners. Is that true?

RUSSELL I should think it's very likely. My brother knew everybody concerned and when the Home Secretary wasn't being very obliging my brother went to see him. Oh, you know – 'He was my fag at Winchester, he'll do it.' So he did.

FREEMAN Now, at the time of your own trial and imprisonment, do you think, looking back, that Trinity College behaved either wisely or justly in depriving you of your Fellowship?

RUSSELL No. Certainly not, especially as they did it while the case was *sub judice*. All the younger Fellows had gone to the war and the government of the college was left to the old boys and the old boys said: 'We must do our bit. We can't fight, we're too old'; and their bit was to get rid of me!

FREEMAN Now, something very similar to that, of course, happened in the Second World War, when your appointment at the College of the City of New York was terminated.

RUSSELL Oh, in the Second World War I was completely patriotic. I supported the war and I was entirely orthodox in my views about that.

FREEMAN Nevertheless, you were thrown out of another college.

RUSSELL Ah, but that was for quite different reasons. That was on the grounds of my views about marriage and morals. That was a Roman Catholic business.

FREEMAN But your views must have been known when you were appointed to the College of the City of New York?

RUSSELL Oh yes; but civilised people didn't mind them. But there was a whole rabble in New York of uneducated Irish people and they had completely absolutely ignorant views. There was a woman who was intending to send her daughter to the College of the City of New York, where her daughter was not going to study mathematical logic, which was the subject I was going to teach; but nevertheless, this woman professed to be afraid that I should rape her daughter or corrupt her in some way by my mere presence in other classrooms in the same university. And on that ground she brought an action that I should be deprived of my position and she accused me of being lewd, lecherous, lascivious, obscene and aphrodisiac. And all of these charges were upheld by the judge in court and the judge said that he would therefore annul this appointment.

FREEMAN Did she bring any evidence to justify these charges?

RUSSELL Yes – oh yes. It was proved that I had said that an infant under six months old if seen touching his parts should not be slapped.

That was the chief evidence.

FREEMAN What happened to you when you lost your job in New York? Did you have another job to go to in America?

RUSSELL No newspaper would print a word I wrote. No magazine would print a word. No hall would allow me to lecture in it. So that I was cut off from all my means of livelihood and I couldn't get any money out of England at that time because of currency regulations and so I was expecting to starve. I had three children whom I was educating, two of them at the university and one younger, and I expected we should all suffer very badly. And we should have done but for a certain man I'll call Dr Barnes, who came to my rescue and gave me a job.

FREEMAN As a result of that alarming experience, have you felt any permanent resentment against the Americans?

RUSSELL Oh no – none whatever.

FREEMAN Do you ever now, in old age, encounter these explosions of anger?

RUSSELL Oh yes. I had a letter from an Anglican bishop not long ago in which he said that all my opinions on everything were inspired by sexual lust. And that the opinions I have expressed on this subject were among the causes of the Second World War.

FREEMAN You said that when you lost your job in New York, you were really anxious about the future. Could I ask you, because it is of interest to the background of the academic life generally, were you left a fortune by your family, or have you earned all you've had all your life?

RUSSELL I was left a certain amount of money. When I came of age I had capital that brought me in about £600 a year and then I became a socialist and I came to the conclusion that I ought not to live on inherited money and I got rid of my capital gradually to various causes which I thought important; and since then I have lived entirely on my earnings.

FREEMAN Which of your activities in your working life has been financially most rewarding?

RUSSELL Oh well, the writing of books. I mean, some of my books have brought in a great deal of money, especially the *History of Western Philosophy*.

FREEMAN Looking back now on all the causes that you've especially championed throughout your working life, do you think your advocacy has been on the whole successful?

RUSSELL My views on what you may call sexual questions have, I think, been immensely successful. I mean, the world has moved that way and to a very great extent on education too; and one of the things that I used to be enormously interested in was equality of women and that, of course, has been completely successful. Also I was from an early time a socialist and there's a great deal of socialism in England now and I'm glad of it. So that I've had a very fair measure of success, but in other things, of course, not at all.

FREEMAN Do you think that on the whole the fanatics in the world are more useful or more dangerous than the sceptics?

RUSSELL I think fanaticism is the gravest danger there is. I might almost say that I was fanatical against fanaticism.

FREEMAN But then are you not fanatical also against some other things? Your current campaign, for instance, in favour of nuclear disarmament; would you encourage your supporters to undertake some of the extreme demonstrations that they undertake? Isn't that fanaticism?

RUSSELL I don't think that's fanaticism, no. I mean, some of them may be fanatical but I support them because everything sane and sensible and quiet that we do is absolutely ignored by the press and the only way we can get into the press is to do something that looks fanatical.

FREEMAN Do you think it is possible that the anti-nuclear campaign may already be a bit out of date in the light of the preparations for bacteriological and biological warfare which we now know are going on?

RUSSELL It certainly would be if it was only a campaign against nuclear weapons; but it is, in fact, a campaign against war. Scientific Man cannot survive if he is going to continue to make war. I mean, the worst possibility is that human life may be extinguished. But assuming that doesn't happen, I can't bear the thought of many hundreds of millions of people dying in agony, only and solely because the rulers of the world are stupid and wicked – and I can't bear it!

FREEMAN Is it true or untrue, that in recent years you advocated that a preventive war might be made against communism, against Soviet Russia?

RUSSELL It's entirely true and I don't repent of it. It was not inconsistent with what I think now. What I thought all along was, that nuclear war in which both sides have nuclear weapons would be an utter and absolute disaster. Now, there was a time just after the last war when the Americans had a monopoly of nuclear weapons and offered to internationalise nuclear weapons by the Baruch proposal; and I thought this an extremely generous proposal on their part, one which it would be very desirable that the world should accept. And I did think that great pressure should be put upon Russia to accept the Baruch proposal and that, if they continued to refuse, it might be necessary actually to go to war. At that time nuclear weapons existed only on one side and therefore the odds were the Russians would have given way.

FREEMAN Just supposing they hadn't given way, would you have been prepared to face the consequences?

RUSSELL Yes.

FREEMAN You would have used these weapons on the Russians in spite of the words you have used to me about their horror?

RUSSELL I should. They were not, of course, nearly as bad as these modern weapons are. I thought then and hoped that the Russians would give way, but of course, you can't threaten unless you are prepared to have your bluff called.

FREEMAN There has, of course, been one good thing come out of all this scientific research into war and that is the conquest of space, don't you see that as a hopeful development?

RUSSELL I don't see it as a hopeful development particularly. I'm charmed with the ingenuity and I'm charmed with the increase of knowledge which it might bring, but when – as is the case – money is only spent in order to spread our silly squabbles throughout the solar system, I find it utterly disgusting.

FREEMAN Do you look back to the nineteenth century on the whole with nostalgia and regret?

RUSSELL Well, it all depends upon what you are thinking about. The world was much more beautiful to look at than it is now. And one thing after another, one piece of beauty after another, is destroyed and that I do profoundly regret; but when it comes to ideas, well, there's immensely less humbug than there was, and that I rejoice in.

FREEMAN And the sort of conventional self-indulgences, or vices, like drink and tobacco and so on, which is your favourite one?

RUSSELL Oh, tobacco. I smoke a pipe all day long except when I am eating or sleeping.

FREEMAN Hasn't that shortened your life?

RUSSELL Well, they used to say it would when I first took to it but I took to it some seventy years ago so it doesn't seem to have had a very great effect, so far. In fact, you know, on one occasion it saved my life. I was in an aeroplane and there was an accident, a bad accident, and all the people in the non-smoking part of the plane were drowned and the people in the smoking part jumped into the Norwegian fjord where we'd landed and were saved. So that I owe my life to smoking.

FREEMAN And did you think great thoughts about death and survival when you were actually swimming?

RUSSELL No. I was rung up by a journalist in Copenhagen and he said: 'What did you think while you were swimming in the fjord?' So I said: 'I thought the water was cold.' And he said: 'Did you not think about mysticism and logic?' And I said: 'No'; and rang off.

FREEMAN Have you, in your eighty-seventh year, any unfulfilled ambitions?

RUSSELL Oh well, of course, there are all sorts of things I should like to have written and haven't written yet. I mean, almost every day I think of some new subject I should like to have written a book about but there isn't time to write them all.

FREEMAN One last question – suppose, Lord Russell, this film were to be looked at by our descendants like a Dead Sea scroll, in a thousand years' time, what would you think it's worth telling that generation about the life you've lived and the lessons you've learnt from it?

RUSSELL I should like to say two things, one intellectual and one moral. The intellectual thing is this. When you are studying any matter or considering any philosophy, ask yourself only what are the facts and what is the truth that the facts bear out. Never let yourself be diverted either by what you would wish to believe or by what you think would have beneficent social effects if it were believed, but look only and surely at what are the facts.

The moral thing is very simple. I should say: Love is wise, hatred is foolish. In this world, which is getting more and more closely interconnected, we have to learn to tolerate each other. We have to learn to put up with the fact that some people say things that we don't like. We can only live together in that way and if we are to live together and not die together, we must learn the kind of charity and the kind of tolerance which is absolutely vital to the continuation of human life on this planet.

DAME EDITH SITWELL

INTRODUCTION

For her interview on the *Face to Face* series, Dame Edith Sitwell wore a head-dress she called her 'bird-king's hat', an ermine jacket and huge, exotic rings on her fingers.

It was May 1959 and Dame Edith was true to form as the eccentric *grande dame* of English letters. She answered interviewer John Freeman's questions with poise and humour; some of them she refused. Freeman in turn was courteous and charming.

Dame Edith was seventy-one at the time of the interview and an extremely well-known poet and personality. Since the 1920s she had been part of a notable, sometimes notorious, literary trio with her brothers, Osbert and Sacheverell. She was and remained a controversial figure; her life was full of literary skirmishes and quite reckless fighting with the academic world and those who were critical of her work. She was an untiring champion of young writers and musicians – Dylan Thomas and William Walton among them. She was loved by the American public, giving triumphant lecture tours and poetry readings over there.

Yet underneath this very public, eccentric figure one has a sense of quite a sad, misunderstood woman, with a strong private sense of purpose and a slowly blossoming charm.

John Freeman said that Dame Edith was the most difficult *Face to Face* guest he had to interview, both because of her very individual way of answering questions and because her rhythms of speech were so unpredictable that he was never sure when she had finished a sentence. The two became great friends and Freeman and his wife visited Dame Edith on her death-bed five years later.

The interview was widely considered to be among the finest of the series. The *Daily Herald* said: 'Here was a living legend captured on the popular screen.' And many people contacted the BBC to say what an insight the programme had been into her character.

Dame Edith once said: 'People frequently loathe me to begin with but it works out all right when we get to know each other.' The *Face to Face* interview made that possible, bringing to a public bemused by her flamboyant style and reputation the true face and presence of one of the most remarkable public figures of the time.

INTERVIEW

FREEMAN Dame Edith, the world outside your own circle of friends tends to think of you as being remote, eccentric, forbidding and rather dangerous. Now, perhaps that's a false impression, and I want you to tell me, face to face, what sort of person you really are. First your appearance, which everybody knows. Why did you devise the very personal style of clothes that you wear so often?

SITWELL Well, because I can't wear fashionable clothes. You see, I'm a throw-back to remote ancestors of mine, and I really would look so extraordinary if I wore coats and skirts. I would be followed for miles and people would doubt the existence of the Almighty if they saw me looking like that.

FREEMAN But is the style that you do wear intended to suggest any particular period?

SITWELL No, it comes naturally. You see, I'm descended from the most queer and remote sources. On one side, my maternal grandmother was the daughter of the Duke of Beaufort of her time, descended straight from the Red Rose Plantagenets, and on another side, I'm descended from an errand boy who walked barefoot from Leeds to London, and built up a large fortune – well, that persistence and grandeur I'm extremely proud of – and the woman who was known as the wicked Lady Conyngham, my great great-grandmother, and who was so wicked that she stopped the flogging in women's prisons. I'm proud of that particular thing.

FREEMAN Well now, tell me about your life today. Where do you live, for instance?

SITWELL I live with my eldest brother Osbert, at Renishaw, in Derbyshire, which is my family home, and for part of the year I go with him to his Italian home, which is Castello di Montegufoni, an extremely romantic house.

FREEMAN And is it a big, grand house like Renishaw?

SITWELL It is, and it belongs to various dates. The tower in it and the great castle wall were built by the Dukes of Athens, the Acciaiuolis, in eleven hundred and something – I always forget the exact date – when the dukes were thrown out of Athens by the Turks, and came to

Montegufoni, where they were not always very hospitable, because if people came out from Florence whom they didn't want to see, they just threw boiling oil on them from the castle walls, you see.

FREEMAN What are your own personal hobbies and relaxations when you're not working?

SITWELL Reading, listening to music, and silence.

FREEMAN Do you like the country better than the town?

SITWELL Oh yes.

FREEMAN What in particular do you like about the country?

SITWELL The quiet. And not being bothered by silly questions.

FREEMAN That's a very successful answer. Are there particular pieces of music which give you special comfort when you're feeling over-strained?

SITWELL I don't know comfort, but excitement. You see, I have been, in my life, very much influenced by the works of Mr Stravinsky.

FREEMAN And would you say he was your favourite composer? If you have to turn to music in a moment of strain, would it be to Stravinsky?

SITWELL No. I suppose that it would be to Bach, and Beethoven, and Mozart. But certainly Mr Stravinsky amongst them, but more for excitement than for being soothed, you see.

FREEMAN Tell me a little now about the way in which you work. Do you, for instance, write your poetry at regular hours, or do you have to sit and wait for inspiration to come upon you?

SITWELL Oh, I sit and wait for inspiration, yes, of course; one is obliged to do that.

FREEMAN Do you work, in fact, a certain number of hours every day, or does waiting for inspiration mean that you often go for weeks without working?

SITWELL No, it doesn't mean that, because if I haven't an inspiration, then I am producing a poet's notebook – quotations from what various poets, various painters and various musicians have said about the arts, which will cast some reflection on poetry.

FREEMAN So that your work you do do at regular hours, even if not poetry?

SITWELL Indeed, yes.

FREEMAN Do you revise your work many times?

SITWELL Oh yes. I will sometimes have almost a whole notebook full of quite a short poem.

FREEMAN Writing many, many drafts?

SITWELL Oh yes.

FREEMAN Dame Edith, have you in fact kept yourself by the rewards of your pen? Or have you had private income to help you all your life?

SITWELL I have an *extremely* small income – but smaller than anyone could think – and I have always earned my own living; I've been excessively poor. I'm always supposed to be extremely rich.

FREEMAN But you really have known poverty?

SITWELL Oh, great poverty.

FREEMAN And what did you do about it? Did you get a job?

SITWELL Well, during the first war – you see, my father was rather an odd old gentleman – and I had to take a job which brought me in twenty-five shillings a week, and two shillings war bonus; and I did that partly out of patriotism, but partly because I was too poor to live without it.

FREEMAN Dame Edith, are you a shy person?

SITWELL Extremely.

FREEMAN Are you enjoying yourself now, or is it torture?

SITWELL I like talking to *you*. I don't always like talking to people, because I am shy of them. If I think I'm boring them, you see, it is dreadful for me. You asked me just now – you said that people's idea of me was that I was eccentric, and savage? –

FREEMAN Forbidding, I said, and dangerous.

SITWELL Well, I don't think I'm forbidding excepting when I absolutely refuse to be taught my job by people who know nothing about it. I have devoted my whole life to writing poetry, which is to me a form of religion, and I'm not going to be taught by people who don't know anything about it. I think it's very impertinent. I mean, I don't teach plumbers how to plumb!

FREEMAN Just so. Well, now I want to take you back to your childhood. It's always said that you had an unhappy childhood?

SITWELL Extremely unhappy.

FREEMAN Why? Because you were a girl?

SITWELL Partly, and also because my father and mother married without knowing anything about life at all. My mother was seventeen and, poor thing, she didn't know anything about life. She was just *made* to marry my father, and they just didn't understand the first thing about each other.

FREEMAN What sort of woman was she?

SITWELL She was very beautiful. She had the most terrible rages, which – Oh, well, I've forgiven her so long ago.

FREEMAN And what about your father? He was a notable eccentric, now. What do you remember –

SITWELL Oh, well, wild eccentric! When I was a child I was fond of him, only between the ages of thirteen and seventeen, because he was then kind to me, but then he suddenly turned round on me; I've never found out why.

FREEMAN Is it, in fact, true that both your parents disliked your appearance as a child?

SITWELL I don't think my mother bothered about it. My father loathed it. He liked people covered with curls and, quite frankly, rather common. You see, he'd married a lady, and it hadn't gone very well, so of course he didn't want any more ladies about.

FREEMAN And is it true that he tried to change your appearance – that he had recourse to plastic surgery?

SITWELL Oh yes.

FREEMAN What happened about that? Tell me.

SITWELL Oh well, it was very dreadful. I don't want to talk about it.

FREEMAN All right. As part of this unhappy childhood, were you punished, or were you teased? What was the particular form of torture?

SITWELL Well, I think they resorted to everything which could possibly humiliate or hurt me.

FREEMAN Including, for instance, spoiling your brothers, at your expense?

SITWELL Well, my brothers would never allow that to happen if they'd known it. You see, my brother Osbert is five years younger than me, my brother Sacheverell is ten years younger than me, and we're an absolutely devoted family – I mean, you couldn't find a more devoted trio, do you see.

FREEMAN Looking back, though, on your childhood, who were the *real* friends that you had at Renishaw, in those days of extreme youth?

SITWELL Well, when I was a small child, my dear old nurse was wonderful, and then there was the fascinating Henry, who came of a long line of whalers, and who was first of all footman and then butler, and he came when I was two years old. He used to button up my shoes, you see, for me, when I was put into a perambulator, and he would always, in after life, come to me and say to me, 'Look out, miss, you'd better get out of the back door because her ladyship's coming for you.'

FREEMAN How much of the ordinary life of the country did you see, living at Renishaw in your childhood? Did you love the animals, for instance?

SITWELL Well, until my brothers were born, my only companions were birds. I loved the wild birds but my pet birds – there was a peacock, you see, and he and I loved each other very much, and I was four years old and he had a kind of feeling for time, he would fly up to the leads outside my mother's bedroom, when I went to say good morning to her, and when he saw me he would give a harsh shriek and at that moment I didn't dislike ugly voices as I'm afraid I do now, and he would then wait for me until I came out again, when he would give another scream and fly down into the garden and wait for me. We would then walk round and round the garden, as you might say, arm in arm, excepting he hadn't any arms; I would have my arm round his neck; and I was asked why I loved him so and I said, 'Because he's proud and has a crown, and is beautiful.' And then my father got him a wife, with his usual tactlessness, after which he never looked at me again, and my heart was broken.

FREEMAN That was your first disillusion, perhaps?

SITWELL My first disillusion.

FREEMAN Was that before or after you ran away from home?

SITWELL Oh, it was before I ran away from home. I ran away from home when I was five, and I couldn't put on my boots, unfortunately, and so I was captured at the end of the street and brought back by a policeman, whom I hit as hard as I could, but I was restored.

FREEMAN Now, when and how did you eventually escape from this closed family circle?

SITWELL Well, when I was twenty-five I was let out on ticket of leave.

FREEMAN Were you given enough money to make the ticket of leave a very rewarding one?

SITWELL Oh no, no. You see, my father lived in the thirteenth century where a groat was quite a lot, you know what I mean.

FREEMAN Yes. Now, have there been any other writers in recent generations in your family?

SITWELL Not in recent generations, no.

FREEMAN Does it strike you as odd that your one generation should produce three writers of such distinction as you and your two brothers? Do you think that any of you would have had the careers you have had if it hadn't been for this extraordinary childhood? Did it help you in the long run?

SITWELL I think it came partly from my father's queer intellectuality and coldness, and from my mother's wild fire, passion and impossible temper.

FREEMAN All your professional life, I have the feeling that you particularly, but your brothers as well, have been campaigning, you've been crusading, either against something or for something.

SITWELL Always *for* something. For any kind of new great work which was coming along. I mean, we have after all found and helped a good many great artists in various arts. We really have, you know. And against cruelty, against injustice, against snobbery.

FREEMAN Well now, it's sometimes said about you, and I'm going to put it to you, that in doing all this you've deliberately courted a great deal of publicity. Is that true or not?

SITWELL I *loathe* publicity! With my brother Osbert's first novel – he happens to have a most magnificent profile, and some person – a critic! I ask you! – writing about the novel, said that he had the profile of a Hottentot. We quoted that. We also quoted, as far as I remember, something said about me – that I was as ugly as modern poetry. It seems to me to have nothing to do with one's work at all, and we quoted those things, not in order to get publicity, but in order to teach people their manners. We thought they might be ashamed. They weren't.

FREEMAN You haven't ever, quite honourably and sensibly, sought to use publicity in order to further the causes that you have at heart?

SITWELL I don't think that I have.

FREEMAN Have you ever tried purposely to avoid it?

SITWELL I have tried in every way to avoid personal publicity – since I was of a certain age. When I was young I didn't care so much.

FREEMAN You have succeeded in attracting a good deal of attention one way and another, even outside your works of poetry. Wouldn't you agree?

SITWELL Yes, but that isn't my fault.

FREEMAN Now, in recent years I suspect that you really have become a member of the establishment, although you enjoy your –

SITWELL *Oh* no, I've not! No, no, no, no. No, no.

FREEMAN How can you be a Dame and not be a member of the establishment?

SITWELL Because it has nothing to do with it. I mean, I shall always be the same kind of poet.

FREEMAN Do you enjoy the honours which have been showered on you?

SITWELL Yes. Intensely.

FREEMAN Now, you have taken – you referred to it yourself a moment ago – a particular pleasure all through your life, I think, in spotting young talent and helping young people on. Is that because you feel you didn't get the help that you required yourself when you were young?

SITWELL No.

FREEMAN Is it just because you like the company of young people particularly?

SITWELL It is because I have a passion for the arts.

FREEMAN Yes, but not necessarily a passion for young people as well? Because you have been particularly diligent, have you not, in seeking out and helping the young?

SITWELL Oh well, I always have a tenderness for the young. But I don't encourage young people because they're young. If somebody of sixty came along who was a genius, I should just as much wish to help him or her.

FREEMAN Do you in fact find it very easy to make close personal friendships, or do they come hard?

SITWELL When I die, I will be able to say that I think that I've given more devotion, and had more devotion, than most people I know.

FREEMAN Have you ever – I hope I may ask this – seriously contemplated marriage?

SITWELL That I think I can't answer.

FREEMAN No reason indeed why you should at all. Do you consider, looking at young people today, so many of whom you've helped, that the standard of taste and behaviour among the young is lower than it used to be? Is this story of the depravity of the beat generation true?

SITWELL Well, you see, I think you said that I was a forbidding old lady – well, I'm very forbidding. No young person would ever dare misbehave themselves in my presence, and I can think of one very great poet who died some time ago – I never once saw him behave in any way that a great man shouldn't behave.

FREEMAN Would you tell me who that was? I can guess, and I think it would be nice for you to –

SITWELL Dylan Thomas.

FREEMAN Dylan Thomas, who was indeed one of the people you very much helped, was he not?

SITWELL Yes. And he behaved always impeccably in my presence.

FREEMAN Now, I want to change the subject and ask you about something quite different, because there was one episode in your career which has puzzled a lot of people. Why did you decide some years ago to go to Hollywood and work in the Hollywood machine?

SITWELL Well, I was not working on poetry at the moment and I needed to earn money.

FREEMAN Did Hollywood either succeed in, or even seek, to lower your standards?

SITWELL Oh, not for a moment!

FREEMAN How did you ward them off, because they have after all corrupted a great many?

SITWELL I didn't have to. I only saw people whose behaviour was impeccable, who were highly educated and the sort of people I would know in England.

FREEMAN Who were the particularly creative and generous characters that you remember from Hollywood?

SITWELL Well, there was George Cukor, who would have been the director of my film if it had been done, and who is a very highly cultivated man, whose friends are all highly cultivated people, and I used to enjoy very greatly going to his house. He was a most delightful and very kind man.

FREEMAN Did you make any personal friends whom you've kept since?

SITWELL Not great personal friends, no.

FREEMAN Is the story of your affection for – or whatever it was – Marilyn Monroe just a press story, or is it true? Did it really happen?

SITWELL Well, I'll tell you what happened exactly. You see, she was brought to see me in Hollywood, and I thought her a very nice girl. I thought that she had been disgracefully treated, most unchivalrously treated. If people have never been poor, perhaps they don't know what it is like to be hungry. That girl allowed a calendar to be made of her, you see. Well, there have been nude models before now. It means nothing against a person's moral character at all. This poor girl was absolutely persecuted by people. I mean she had an unfortunate attraction for an extremely unpleasant kind of man, whom she avoided assiduously – I have seen her do that, when she was brought to see me. I really did, you see. I mean she behaved like a lady.

FREEMAN Now, you do visit America pretty regularly nowadays and I want to ask you, do you find that the American way of life is a good one for an artist?

SITWELL Oh yes.

FREEMAN Why?

SITWELL Well, there are certain comforts which prevent you from being harassed the whole time. That, I think, is a very good thing. I mean, everybody excepting the very, very poor have ice-boxes, and have motors, and –

FREEMAN Yes, but with all that mechanisation, and all the sort of speed which accompanies it, did you not find that the contemplation which is necessary for your work rather disappears?

SITWELL No, I've always been able to work perfectly.

FREEMAN And do the Americans treat artists with the respect that is their due?

SITWELL Oh, my goodness me, yes! They're perfectly wonderful audiences. They're so kind. I mean, for instance, after we had had a performance somewhere or other, our photographs were put in the paper; and a week afterwards some young people saw my eldest brother and me standing on a street corner waiting for a taxi, and they ran and got a taxi for us!

FREEMAN Do you want to be unrecognised as you go about your life?

SITWELL I want, frankly, not for people to come up and bother me about every kind of trivial thing.

FREEMAN Has it ever occurred to you that if you did just once dress like Garbo in an old mackintosh and a slouch hat you would go unrecognised?

SITWELL No. I shouldn't.

FREEMAN You'd rather not pay that price for it?

SITWELL I should hate to do it; I don't see why I should because people are impertinent!

FREEMAN Is it your experience that on the whole people are impertinent with the public figures whom they know well and love?

SITWELL Not everybody. Some are most considerate, but some are extremely impertinent. I mean, anybody thinks that they have a perfect right to come up and bother me about their own problems.

FREEMAN Somebody did once write about you, Dame Edith, 'It's not what she writes but what she *is* exerts the real fascination', and that's what I've been trying to find out tonight. Now, before I give you the last word, I want you to listen to three most lovely lines, which I quote from one of your own poems:
    The great sins and fires break out of me
    Like the terrible leaves from the bough in the violent spring . . .
    I am a walking fire, I am all leaves.
Dame Edith, what is that great fire? What is the living thing which all your life has been trying to break out of you?

SITWELL The great fire, I suppose, is a humble but unworthy love of God, and certainly a great love of humanity. And to be an artist is a terribly painful thing. I mean, the great leaves break out of me – you see, one has a perpetual resurrection in one's life, as the art returns to one, after long deadness. And of course the fire's always fighting the sins, and – Well, there one is.

CARL GUSTAV JUNG

INTRODUCTION

Carl Gustav Jung was eighty-four years old when he was interviewed for the BBC series *Face to Face* in October 1959. At the time he was the world's greatest living psychologist, founder of analytical psychology and originator of the concept of the collective unconscious. So his agreeing to be interviewed was a historic coup; indeed, he was arguably John Freeman's most famous guest ever to appear in the series.

The programme itself did not follow the usual studio format. A film team flew to Jung's Zurich home. And as well as seeing the old man walking by the lakeside, viewers were also given a glimpse of the usually shadowy, somewhat enigmatic John Freeman himself, whose face, despite the programme's title, rarely appeared on the screen.

And another difference: of all the thirty-five *Face to Face* guests, Jung was the only one to refuse to have his portrait drawn by Felix Topolski. What would an analyst make of that?

At the time of the interview Jung was still working, his mind still sharp, his concentration focused. It was a timely interview; eighteen months later Jung was dead.

Freeman's shrewdly balanced questions about the life and about the work create a rounded portrait of one of the greatest men of his day. Of them all this *Face to Face* is a part of history.

INTERVIEW

FREEMAN Professor Jung, how many years have you lived in this lovely house by the lake at Zurich?

JUNG It's just about fifty years.

FREEMAN No children or grandchildren with you?

JUNG Oh no, they don't live here, but I have plenty of them in the surroundings.

FREEMAN Do they come to see you often?

JUNG Oh yes!

FREEMAN How many grandchildren have you?

JUNG Oh, nineteen.

FREEMAN And great-grandchildren?

JUNG I think eight and I suppose one is on the way.

FREEMAN And do you enjoy having them?

JUNG Well, of course, it's nice to feel such a living crowd are out of oneself.

FREEMAN Are they afraid of you, do you think?

JUNG I don't think so. If you would know my grandchildren you wouldn't think so! They steal my things. Even my hat that belongs to me they stole the other day.

FREEMAN Now, can I take you back to your own childhood. Do you remember the occasion when you first felt consciousness of your own individual self?

JUNG That was in my eleventh year. Suddenly, on my way to school, it was just as if I had been walking in a mist, and I stepped out of it and I knew: I am. I am what I am. And then I thought: But what have I been before? And then I found that I had been in a mist, not knowing how to differentiate myself from things. I was just one thing among many things.

FREEMAN What memories have you of your parents? Were they strict and old-fashioned in the way they brought you up?

JUNG Oh well, you know, they belonged to the later part of the Middle Ages, and my father was a parson in the country, and you can imagine what people were then, you know, in the seventies of the past century; they had the convictions in which people have lived since one thousand eight hundred years.

FREEMAN How did he try to impress these convictions on you? Did he punish you, for instance?

JUNG Oh no, not at all, no. He was very liberal, and he was most tolerant and most understanding.

FREEMAN Which did you get on with more intimately, your father or your mother?

JUNG That's difficult to say. Of course, one is always more intimate with the mother, but when it comes to the personal feeling I had a better relation to my father, who was predictable, than with my mother, who was to me a very problematical something.

FREEMAN So at any rate fear was not an element in your relation with your father?

JUNG Not at all.

FREEMAN Did you accept him as being infallible in his judgements?

JUNG Oh no, I knew he was very fallible.

FREEMAN How old were you when you knew that?

JUNG Now, let me see. Perhaps eleven or twelve years old. It was hanging together with the fact that I knew I *was*, and from then on I saw that my father was different.

FREEMAN Yes. So the moment of self-revelation was closely connected with realising the fallibility of your parents?

JUNG Yes, one could say so. I realised that I had fear of my mother, but not during the day. Then she was quite known to me, and predictable, but in the night I had fear of my mother.

FREEMAN And can you remember why?

JUNG I have not the slightest idea why.

FREEMAN What about your schooldays, now? Were you happy at school?

JUNG It was wonderful to have company; but soon, you know, in a country school naturally I was far ahead – and then I began to be bored.

FREEMAN What sort of religious upbringing did your father give you?

JUNG Oh, we were Swiss Reformed.

FREEMAN And did he make you attend church regularly?

JUNG Oh, that was quite natural. Everybody went to church on Sunday.

FREEMAN Yes. And did you believe in God?

JUNG Oh yes.

FREEMAN Do you now believe in God?

JUNG Now? Difficult to answer. I *know*. I don't need to believe. I know.

FREEMAN Well now, what made you decide to become a doctor?

JUNG Originally I wanted to be an archaeologist; Assyriology, Egyptology, or something of the sort. I hadn't the money; the study was too expensive. So my second love then belonged to nature, particularly zoology, and when I began my studies I inscribed in the so-called philosophical faculty, too – that means natural sciences – but then I soon saw that the career that was before me would make a schoolmaster of me, you see.

I didn't want to become a schoolmaster. Teaching was not just what I was looking for, and so I remembered that my grandfather had been a doctor, and I knew that when I was studying medicine I had a chance to study natural science and to become a doctor, and a doctor can develop, you see, he can have a practice, he can choose his scientific interests more or less. At all events I would have more chance than being a schoolmaster, also the idea of doing something useful with human beings appealed to me.

FREEMAN And did you, when you decided to become a doctor, have difficulty in getting the training at school and in passing the exams?

JUNG I particularly had a difficulty with certain teachers. I remember one case where the teacher had the custom, the habit, to discuss the papers written by the pupils, and he took the best first, and he went through the whole number of the pupils and I didn't appear, and I was badly troubled over it, and I thought, Well, it is impossible that my thesis can be *that* bad, and when he had finished he said: 'There is still one paper left over and that is the one by Jung. That would be by far the best paper if it hadn't been copied. You are a thief, you! And if I knew where you had stolen it I would fling you out of school!' And I got mad and said this is the one thesis where I have worked the most, because the theme was interesting, in contradistinction, you know, to other themes which are not at all interesting to me, and then he said: 'You are a liar, and if we can prove that you have stolen that thing somewhere, then you get out of school.' And I hated that fellow, and that was the only man I could have killed, you know, if I had met him once at a dark corner!

FREEMAN Did you often have violent thoughts about people when you were young?

JUNG No, not exactly. Only when I got mad. Well, then I beat them up. Once I was attacked by about seven boys and I got mad, and I took one, and just swung him round with his legs, you know, and beat down four of them, and then they were satisfied.

FREEMAN And were there any consequences from that afterwards?

JUNG Oh, I should say, yes! From then on I was always suspected that I was at the bottom of every trouble. I was not, but they were afraid and I was never attacked again.

FREEMAN Well now, when the time came that you qualified as a doctor, what made you decide to specialise in being an alienist?

JUNG Well, that is rather an interesting point. When I had finished my studies practically and when I didn't know what I really wanted to do, I had a big chance to follow one of my professors – he was called to a new position in Munich, and he wanted me as his assistant, but then in that moment I studied for my final examination, I came across a textbook of psychiatry. Up to then I thought nothing about it, because our professor then wasn't particularly interested, and I only read the introduction to that book, where certain things were said, about psychosis as a maladjustment of the personality. That hit the nail on the head. I saw I must become an alienist. My heart was thumping wildly in that moment, and when I told my professor I wouldn't follow him, I would study psychiatry, he couldn't understand it. Nor my friends, because in those days psychiatry was nothing, nothing at all. But I saw the one great chance to unite certain contrasting things in myself, namely, beside natural science I always had studied history of philosophy and such subjects. It was just as if suddenly two streams were joining.

FREEMAN And how long was it after you took that decision that you first came in contact with Freud?

JUNG I'd finished my studies in 1900 and in 1907 I became acquainted with him personally.

FREEMAN Will you tell me how that happened? Did you go to Vienna to meet him?

JUNG Oh well, then I'd written a book about the psychology of dementia praecox, schizophrenia then. And I sent him that book, and thus became acquainted. I went to Vienna for a fortnight and then we had a very long and penetrating conversation, and that settled it.

FREEMAN And what sort of man was Freud?

JUNG Well, he was a complicated nature, you know. I liked him very much, but I soon discovered that when he had thought something then it was settled, while I was doubting all along the line, and it was impossible to discuss something really *au fond*. You know he had no philosophical education, so from the very beginning there was a discrepancy.

FREEMAN Did you in fact grow apart later, partly because of a difference in temperamental approach to experiment and proof and so on?

JUNG Well, of course, there is always a temperamental difference, and his approach was naturally different from mine because his personality was different from mine. That led me into my later investigation of psychological types, with definite attitudes; some people are doing it in this way and other people are doing it in another *typical* way, and there were such differences between myself and Freud, too.

FREEMAN Do you consider that Freud's standard of proof and experimentation was less high than your own?

JUNG Well, you see, that is an evaluation I'm not competent of; I am not my own history, or my historiograph. With reference to certain results, I think my method has its merits.

FREEMAN Tell me, did Freud himself ever analyse you?

JUNG Oh yes, I submitted quite a lot of my dreams to him.

FREEMAN And he to you? Yes. Do you remember now at this distance of time what were the significant features of Freud's dreams that you noted at the time?

JUNG Well, that is rather indiscreet to ask. There is such a thing as a professional secret.

FREEMAN He's been dead these many years.

JUNG Yes, but these regards last longer than life. I prefer not to talk about it.

FREEMAN Well now, can we move on to the time when you did eventually part company with Freud. It was partly, I think, with the publication of your book *The Psychology of the Unconscious*. Is that correct?

JUNG That was the real cause. No, I mean the final cause, because it had a long preparation. You know, from the beginning I had a *Reservation mentalisch*; I couldn't agree with quite a number of his ideas.

FREEMAN Which ones in particular?

JUNG Well, chiefly his purely personal approach, and his disregard of the historical conditions of man. You see, we depend largely upon our history. We are shaped through education, through the influence of the parents, which are by no means always personal. They were prejudiced, or they were influenced by historical ideas or what are called dominants, and that is a most decisive factor in psychology. We are not of today or of yesterday; we are of an immense age.

FREEMAN Was it not partly your observation, your clinical observation, of psychotic cases which led you to differ from Freud on this?

JUNG It was partly my experience with schizophrenic patients that led me to the idea of certain general historical conditions. I went even to Washington to study Negroes at the psychiatric clinic there, in order to find out whether they had the same type of dreams as we have, and these experiences and others led me then to the hypothesis that there is an impersonal stratum in our psyche. We had a patient in the ward; he was quiet but completely dissociated, a schizophrenic, and he was in the clinic or the ward twenty years. A little clerk and with no particular education. And once I came into the ward and he was obviously excited and called to me, took me by the lapel of my coat, and led me to the window, and say: 'Doctor! Now! Now you will see. Now look at it. Look up at the sun and see how it moves. See, you must move your head, too, like this, and then you will see the phallus of the sun, and you know, that's the origin of the wind, and you see how the sun moves as you move your head, from one side to the other!' Of course, I did not understand it at all. I thought, Oh, there you are, he's just crazy. But that case remained in my mind, and four years later I came across a paper written by the German historian, Dieterich, who had dealt with the so-called Mithras Liturgy, a part of the great Parisian source of papyrus . . . it had said there: 'After the second prayer you will see the disc of the sun unfold, and you will see hanging down from it the tube, the origin of the wind, and when you move your face to the regions of the east it will move there, and if you move your face to the regions of the west it will follow you.' And instantly I knew now, this is it. This is the vision of my patient.

FREEMAN But how could you be sure that your patient wasn't unconsciously recalling something that somebody had told him?

JUNG Oh no. Quite out of the question, because that thing was not known. It was in a magic papyrus in Paris, and it wasn't even published. It was only published four years later, after I had observed it with my patient.

FREEMAN And this you felt proved that there was an unconscious which was something more than personal?

JUNG Oh well, that was not a proof to me, but it was a hint, and I took the hint.

FREEMAN Now tell me, how did you first decide to start your work on the psychological types? Was that also as a result of some particular clinical experience?

JUNG Less so. It was a very personal reason, namely to find my own bearings.

FREEMAN Have you concluded what psychological type you are yourself?

JUNG Naturally I have devoted a great deal of attention to that painful question, you know! The type is nothing static. It changes in the course of life, but I most certainly was characterised by thinking. I always thought, from early childhood on, and I had a great deal of intuition too, and I had a definite difficulty with feeling, and my relation to reality was not particularly brilliant. I was often at variance with the reality of things. Now, that gives you all the necessary data for a diagnosis!

FREEMAN During the 1930s, when you were working a lot with German patients, you did I believe forecast that a second world war was very likely. Well now, looking at the world today, do you feel that a third world war is likely?

JUNG I have no definite indications in that respect, but there are so many indications that one doesn't know what one sees. People's dreams contain apprehensions, you know, but it is very difficult to say whether they point to a war, because that idea is uppermost in people's mind. Formerly, you know, it has been much simpler. People didn't think of a war, and therefore it was rather clear what the dreams meant. Nowadays no more so. We are so full of apprehensions, fears, that one doesn't know exactly to what it points. One thing is sure. A great change of our psychological attitude is imminent. That is certain.

FREEMAN Now why?

JUNG Because we need more psychology. We need more understanding of human nature, because the only real danger that exists is man itself. His psyche should be studied, because we are the origin of all coming evil.

FREEMAN Well, does man, do you think, need to have the concept of sin and evil to live with? Is this part of our nature?

JUNG Well, obviously.

FREEMAN And of a redeemer?

JUNG That is an inevitable consequence.

FREEMAN This is not a concept which will disappear as we become more rational; it's something which –

JUNG Well, I don't believe that man will ever deviate from the original pattern of his being. There will always be such ideas.

FREEMAN You have written, at one time and another, some sentences which have surprised me a little, about death. Now, in particular I remember you said that death is psychologically just as important as birth and like it it's an integral part of life. But surely it can't be like birth if it's an end, can it?

JUNG Quite honestly, one cannot be quite certain about it, because, you know, there are these peculiar faculties of the psyche, that it isn't entirely confined to space and time; you can have dreams or visions of the future, you can see around corners and such things. Only ignorance denies these facts, you know; it's quite evident that they do exist, and have existed always. Now these facts show that the psyche, in part at least, is not dependent upon these confinements. And then what? When the psyche is not under that obligation to live in time and space alone, and obviously it doesn't, then to that extent the psyche is not subjected to those laws, and that means a practical continuation of life, of a sort of psychical existence beyond time and space.

FREEMAN Do you yourself believe that death is probably the end, or –

JUNG The word belief is a difficult thing for me. I don't believe. I must have a reason for a certain hypothesis. Either I know a thing, and then I know it – I don't need to believe it – I don't allow myself, for instance, to believe a thing just for the sake of believing it. I can't believe it, but when there are sufficient reasons for a certain hypothesis, I shall accept . . . naturally, and I should say: 'We had to reckon with the possibility of so and so' – you know.

FREEMAN Well now, you've told us that we should regard death as being a goal . . .

JUNG Yes.

FREEMAN . . . and that to shrink away from it is to evade life and make life purposeless.

JUNG Yes.

FREEMAN What advice would you give to people in their later life to enable them to do this, when most of them must in fact believe that death is the end of everything?

JUNG I have treated many old people and it's quite interesting to watch what the unconscious is doing with the fact that it is apparently threatened with a complete end. It disregards it. Life behaves as if it were going on, and so I think it is better for old people to live on – to look forward to the next day, as if he had to spend centuries, and then he lives properly. But when he is afraid, when he doesn't look forward, he looks back, he petrifies, he gets stiff and he dies before his time; but when he's living on, looking forward to the great adventure that is ahead, then he lives, and that is about what the unconscious is intending to do.

FREEMAN As the world becomes more technically efficient it seems increasingly necessary for people to behave communally and collectively. Now do you think it possible that the highest development of man may be to submerge his own individuality in a kind of collective consciousness?

JUNG That's hardly possible. A reaction will set in against this communal dissociation. You know, when I think of my patients, they all seek their own existence and to assure their existence against that complete atomisation into nothingness, or into meaninglessness. Man cannot stand a meaningless life.

HENRY MOORE

INTRODUCTION

Of the guest on *Face to Face* on 21 February 1960, his biographer writes: 'With his shortish, stocky physique, ruddy countryman's complexion and tweedy taste in clothes, he might have been a well-to-do Yorkshire farmer.' In fact the guest that night was a man widely considered to be the greatest sculptor of the twentieth century: Henry Moore.

It had not been possible to lure this modest and reticent man into the BBC's studios, and the interview had therefore been conducted at the artist's home in Much Hadham, Hertfordshire. The biographical preamble revealed that Moore was set on being a sculptor from childhood, his interest fostered by his art teacher Alice Gostick with whom he still kept in touch. After excelling at art school, his work was brought to public attention at his first one-man show in London in 1928. Nearly twenty years later, his first large-scale retrospective exhibition was held at New York's Museum of Modern Art, and when he won the main sculpture prize at the Venice Biennale in 1948 he was at last acknowledged as a central influence in contemporary art.

Moore's sculptures are generous, maternal and powerful. The recurrent portrayal of the female figure and of the mother and child image he attributed to an intense attachment to his own mother. He was also greatly influenced by primitive – especially Mexican – and classical art, and by landscape: and many of his figures seem at home in outdoor rural settings. Much of his more 'abstract' work (a description Moore always denied) incorporates holes in an effort to explore three-dimensionality.

Though Moore won many prestigious 'commissions' – he preferred to call them purchases – his work inevitably attracted much controversy, criticism and even physical assault.

Indeed, it was in the hope of learning how better to understand and appreciate Moore's work that many watched his *Face to Face* interview. The viewers' verdict was largely favourable: Moore came over as endearing, modest, sincere and homely, 'as solid as the rock he carves'.

Moore continued to work well into his eighties, his Hertfordshire home by now equipped with many studios and surrounded by acres of parkland graced by his sculptures. When he died in 1986, the *Daily Telegraph* called him 'the most internationally acclaimed of Englishmen, honoured by every civilised country in the world'.

INTERVIEW

FREEMAN Mr Moore, I want you to cast your mind right back and tell me when it first occurred to you that you'd like to be a sculptor?

MOORE I think I was probably about eleven. I remember quite clearly the instant. As a boy, at school, I liked the art lessons, I liked drawing, but the little incident that clinches the thing in my mind was our parents used to send me and my younger sister to Sunday school on Sunday afternoons, to get rid of us, I think, mainly, and the superintendent every Sunday used to give a talk about some little moral, would always have a point to the talk. And one Sunday he told us about Michelangelo carving the head of an old faun in the streets of Florence, and that a passer-by after watching two or three minutes said to Michelangelo, 'But an old faun wouldn't have all its teeth in.' Michelangelo immediately, said the superintendent, took his chisel, knocked out two of the teeth, and there, he said, was a great man listening to the advice of other people even though he didn't know them. Now, this story didn't stick in my mind for its moral but merely that there was someone, Michelangelo, a great sculptor. This just pinpointed something in my mind and I knew from then onwards.

FREEMAN What's your earliest memory of *seeing* sculpture?

MOORE I remember a church at Methley, about two miles from our home, a Gothic church, I think, between 1300 and 1400, and these I drew as a little boy of nine or ten and always looked at them when I went to visit my aunt. That's about the earliest.

FREEMAN Well now, what about your first serious lessons in art? When did they take place?

MOORE When I went to grammar school, and we had an art teacher, a Miss Gostick, half French, and she was wonderfully enthusiastic about the art lessons. Most of the boys and girls didn't seem to care about it, but it was the one lesson of the week that I looked forward to. She was wonderfully helpful in asking one every Sunday to tea, showed me copies of colour magazines and so on – in fact I owe a great deal to her enthusiasm.

FREEMAN Did she remain a friend in after life? Is she alive?

MOORE Today, she's eighty-seven or something like that. Still writes to me and I think is quite proud of the help she gave.

FREEMAN Now, your father was a miner, wasn't he? Did you ever think of going down the pits yourself?

MOORE Never. Because by the time I came along, one brother and two sisters – I was the seventh – had already become teachers, and this path was the one carved out for the rest of the family.

FREEMAN Does that mean that there was enough money by that time that you didn't have to go down the pits?

MOORE No, it was that my father really was a remarkable man. Very ambitious for us children, and had taught himself, although I was told that he had no schooling and earned his living first of all at nine, as in his youth I think there was very little public education, and by the time I remember him very clearly he could help me in my homework from the grammar school. He seemed to know the whole of his Shakespeare, he knew his Bible pretty thoroughly and he taught himself enough trigonometry, mathematics and so on to pass his exam as a manager for the coal mine.

FREEMAN Was he the boss in the family, or was your mother?

MOORE He was absolute boss, a complete Victorian tyrant.

FREEMAN Did you get on with him well?

MOORE Yes, I did. But at the same time one had to keep away from his chair in the corner of the room, because we all were in one room, I remember, and one's homework, everything else, was done on the kitchen table after the meal was cleared away, but his little corner was absolutely sacrosanct. Nobody was allowed to nudge him or bump him in any way whatever.

FREEMAN Did you ever have the feeling that you had to look upon your mother as a sort of protector against your father?

MOORE No. No, I didn't. I just had this great respect for Father. I knew that his opinions had real foundation. For instance, when I came to want to be an artist, he said, 'First become qualified as a teacher like your brother and sisters have done and then change to art if you wish, I mean, be sure that you have some living in your hand.' Well, this was very intelligent and very sensible, but by the time I got to that age I knew that I wasn't going to be a teacher, that I was going to study art.

FREEMAN Well now, how did that happen? Because there must be a big jump from the grammar school, with a talent for art, to actually going to art school and taking it up seriously.

MOORE Well again, this Miss Gostick was a tremendous help. She knew that there were scholarships to be won, to Leeds School of Art, and she'd got me entered for such when I was finishing about seventeen, in the grammar school, but the war came along and I joined at eighteen, but then had the luck, as they did in the First World War, making army grants, and I had one of these when I came out of the army at twenty and went straight to Leeds School of Art.

FREEMAN And was the grant enough to keep you going?

MOORE The grant was about eighty pounds a year and in those days that was plenty, yes.

FREEMAN Where could one now find your first work?

MOORE The first commission that I did was a figure on the Underground building, St James's, and the architect of the building was a man named Charles Holden, and he asked me to do this. At that time I didn't want to do any commissions. I had this feeling that architectural sculpture was bad and I thought that it stopped a sculptor from developing in his own way. However, he behaved like a father to me and after a lot of persuasion got me to do it. Epstein was doing two figures down below, and Gill was carving other of the reliefs.

FREEMAN Yes, and this of course was very much later than the time we have been talking about. I wondered whether by any chance there's anything in your Yorkshire village which dates from this very early period?

MOORE When the war began, I was still then only – what? – fifteen, and it was decided to have a school Roll of Honour for the old students who were joining up, and I carved a scroll and a little scene on the top of it. This was the first real start of one's proper carving career.

FREEMAN And that's still there?

MOORE That I believe is still there.

FREEMAN Now, how old were you when you got married? Were you a student still?

MOORE No, I was then thirty.

FREEMAN But probably in pretty economically straitened conditions still?

MOORE I was very lucky. Straight from being a student I was put on to the staff of the Royal College of Art, and for that I think I got £200 a year for two days a week, and this one got married on, and before being married that £200 was wealth.

FREEMAN Now, I'd like to ask you a bit about the economics of a sculptor's life – not so much your own personal finances as how a young sculptor manages – because before you carve a great piece of stone presumably you've got to buy it. It's not like a painter paying for a canvas – it must cost a good deal of money.

MOORE Well, that is so. A sculptor is handicapped economically and young sculptors can't get their work cast into bronze. Bronze casting is a very expensive thing. In my case I used to go round to the stone yards – the stonemason's – and take odd bits which had been knocked off other pieces, random blocks, they're called, and these I'd store in my studio, and then as one got an idea that fitted one particular piece you could use it.

FREEMAN What is the sort of price you have to pay for one of these huge blocks of stone that you chip away?

MOORE The stone for the Unesco sculpture was over £3000, but that was a huge carving, much much bigger than anything I've done or ever will do again. Marble can be anything from £5 to £6 a cubic foot.

FREEMAN Yes. And the young sculptor before he can count on getting enough commissions, however he manages to scrounge his stone, has to do it pretty economically and pretty cheaply, and speculatively?

MOORE Yes. Oh, I've had young sculptors who have stopped working because they can't afford the price of a bag of plaster.

FREEMAN And then the cost of transportation presumably also is heavy, isn't it?

MOORE Again, the transport is a problem. There's one figure of mine, a reclining stone figure, which was the biggest I'd done up to then, which almost made one bankrupt by having to send it out to exhibitions and pay for transport and get it back.

FREEMAN Do you have to search far and wide to find the materials that you want to work on?

MOORE Not nowadays. I did to begin with. I made a point in the early stages of trying to find as many different English stones which could be carved as possible. I think I did discover some eight or nine stones which ordinarily haven't been used but which I think are very fine stones for carving.

FREEMAN In the Second World War did you find that there was a big interruption of supplies?

MOORE Well, by then I had stone in stock, but what stopped me doing sculpture then, which it did, was the uncertain situation of England, because I thought at that period of taking up munition tool-making, in answer to some appeal. For a year or a year and a half I did no sculpture, doing shelter drawings as a war artist.

FREEMAN And that was in fact a contribution to the war effort rather than an artistic decision?

MOORE No. I'd already begun doing shelter drawings and then was asked to continue with them as a war artist.

FREEMAN I take it that nowadays you're fully occupied with the commissions that you've got?

MOORE No, not at all. I hate commissions. I much prefer for someone to come along and find what I'm doing will suit some particular purpose and use it in that way.

FREEMAN Do you find, as other great sculptors have done in the past, that you can make use of assistants to do some of the rough work before you start in on a piece of stone yourself?

MOORE Oh yes. Now I do. I have one full-time assistant and two other young sculptors who come part of their time. To begin with I was entirely alone, but after one's learnt all the things you need to know about actually doing a job yourself, there are many things in sculpture which is purely straightforward intelligent work for someone to help you.

FREEMAN And these assistants are young people, are they, who are learning?

MOORE They're always young sculptors who have either done four or five years already in schools of art or even sometimes longer, and who then ask to come to me, and some come for three months and stay three years, some come for six months and stay a year and so on.

FREEMAN You live here in a very English village and your work must be very different from anybody else who lives hereabout. Did you get on well with the villagers?

MOORE Yes, I think one met them all in the pub on a Sunday.

FREEMAN Do they think of you as an extraordinary local figure, or do they appreciate your work, or regard you just as an eccentric?

MOORE I hope that they just accept me as someone who works.

FREEMAN Have you ever been put off at any time in your career by the really vicious public outcry which the work of sculptors sometimes attracts?

MOORE No. There was one outcry against my first exhibition at the Leicester Galleries, a criticism that appeared in what was then I think the *Morning Post*, and this said that it was wrong for someone like me to be teaching the young. It could have meant losing one's livelihood, and for a short time I was rather upset by this, but since then I've learnt that the kind of press – I don't mean the serious art critics –

FREEMAN You've learnt to ignore the violent stuff? Have you ever had your work tarred and feathered, as Epstein did?

MOORE Oh yes. Just recently, in Germany, it happened. Just the work of silly hooligans. It's better to ignore those things. And even if something does happen and the press rings me up I pretend I don't know about it. That's the best way out of it.

FREEMAN Well now, I'd like to ask you, following that, a few questions about what it is that you have tried to express in your work. Now, I suppose most people, thinking of your sculpture, would instantly think of a large piece of stone with a hole in it. What is this great emphasis you've placed on the making of holes in stone?

MOORE Well, this was merely a logical development, a furthering, of one's attempt, in my case, to understand form, which is what a sculptor's life is built around, to try to know what actual, three-dimensional reality is like. This is something which you've got to do by steps and stages, that is, to try to know what the back of a thing is like when you're looking at the front of it, to try to know, if I'm looking at you now, what your head, what shape it displaces in space, just what sort of angle it's at with your body. I found that in the attempt to penetrate from one side of a sculpture, of a piece of stone, to the other, by making a hole, as it were . . . this is a chalk pebble that I played about a bit on, and immediately, when you see this side, it makes you guess what the other side is like. Often the other side is different, but you do have this connection. Also too in my case the hole became as important as a shape, as the actual material that surrounded it. The holes were an attempt to understand form.

FREEMAN You've also come again and again to the reclining figure throughout your career. What's the particular significance of that?

MOORE This I wouldn't know. It is a subject which, for me, is unending, and if I had five lifetimes I wouldn't exhaust the possibilities in this theme. It may be that it also connects the human figure with landscape more easily than a standing figure could, and landscape is one of my great obsessions, besides the human figure, and I think it's a way of the two being amalgamated.

FREEMAN Now, it often seems, looking at your work, that you will carve the body perhaps of a reclining figure, or of a standing figure, in massive proportions and then you will somehow distort it by putting a very small and misshapen head on top, and this again is a recurring theme. Why?

MOORE Yes. I think I know what you mean. Some people say, or have said, why do I make the heads so unimportant. Actually, for me the head is the most important part of a piece of sculpture. It gives to the rest a scale, it gives to the rest a certain human poise, and meaning, and it's because I think that the head is so important that often I reduce it in size to make the rest more monumental. The heads of Michelangelo's figures will sometimes go, instead of the usual six and a half, which is the average, will go twelve times. It is a recognised thing.

FREEMAN You seem to me to have two quite different moods and sometimes you carve or mould these great massive and, in human terms, somewhat distorted figures, and on other occasions you do work which is frankly humanist, such as, for instance, the Madonna and Child at Northampton. Is there some totally different feeling in your own mind when you approach these two different kinds of work?

MOORE Yes, in a way there is. Sometimes I do do things which are more – I don't know what word to use – probably more tender in their point of view, in their expression of the human figure, but other times, mostly, it's a power. What appealed to me as a young man about Mexican sculpture was its terrific strength, its terrific stony tension and vitality, and this is really the ideal that I have in sculpture. But at the same time I think that every person's nature has to have both sides to even appreciate one side.

FREEMAN Reflecting on these opposites, do you find that you can work on both kinds simultaneously, because, after all, the period of gestation for these things is pretty long and you presumably change mood while you're at work on them?

MOORE Yes, I think one can.

FREEMAN Well now, let me put a final question to you. Many modern artists, and you certainly, have been clearly out of touch with the ordinary popular public mood for most of your working career. Now then, is therefore your work a form of escapism, or is it perhaps an expression of despair with the state of the world, or is it even some secret joy of your own?

MOORE No, I've never worried much about the communication between the artist and the general public. I've believed that given an opportunity the average person will learn to appreciate sculpture or painting if he's only given the chance, and it seems to me silly for a sculptor to expect the average person, who perhaps has never been to the British Museum, perhaps has never seen a real piece of sculpture in his life, to immediately understand what he's trying to do. It will come about, this connection will come about, through more chance of the average public to see sculpture.

STIRLING MOSS

INTRODUCTION

The programme file for one particular *Face to Face*, in summer 1960, reveals some anxiety on the part of its producer that the desired guest should appear without delay. Among the reasons listed is the warning 'he is likely to be killed soon'. The guest was racing driver Stirling Moss, so far lucky to have escaped a number of occasions on which he had left the road unexpectedly, his car had somersaulted, wheels had come off and rivals' cars had leaped over him.

The British public admired Moss's courage, determination and – too often – position as underdog. He represented a world of undeniable glamour; as one journalist wrote, 'the pushed-up goggles and tired oil-streaked grin could be that of a Battle of Britain fighter pilot just back from an afternoon's dicing with death'.

The son of a dentist who, in his younger days, had also been a racing driver, Moss was always more interested in cars and show-jumping than in his schoolwork. His first idol was the world champion Giuseppe Farina, whose nonchalant straight-arm driving position he adopted; later his master became Juan Manuel Fangio. Sports car racing was his speciality and he was the first Englishman to win the British Grand Prix (doing so ten times altogether), although he never won the World Championship.

Stirling Moss's dedication to the sport and his intense concentration during races – as well as the deaths of many of his friends – were largely responsible for the break-up of his first marriage. In later years he was to marry twice more. His motor racing career was not, however, to end in the way he had suggested to John Freeman. On Easter Monday 1962, a horrifying 140-m.p.h. crash at Goodwood catapulted him into early retirement. Although he refrained from competitions (apart from a couple of brief comebacks some twenty years later), Moss is still involved in many facets of the business – including property development, lecturing and public relations.

This *Face to Face* interview was considered by many to be outstanding. Moss was seen as intelligent, candid and a good television personality. Whether racing fans or not, viewers were delighted to be able to satisfy their curiosity about what makes a racing driver tick.

INTERVIEW

FREEMAN Stirling Moss, the really vital difference between your job and mine and most other people's is that if we make a mistake, well, we perhaps lose a contract or get into trouble with the critics, if you make a mistake you probably lose your life. Now, do you think about death while you're driving in races?

MOSS No, not when I'm driving, but I am frightened of death, if you're not frightened of an accident then what is your limitation? When I'm driving round, of course, unless I overdo it and go too fast – then I certainly am frightened and very conscious of what I've done, you get a sort of tingling of the hands and a feeling as though you've just eaten a lot of porridge which goes right down, you know, to your feet! And that's the sort of sensation I get; but I wouldn't ponder on the thought.

FREEMAN It's fear, in other words, after the event. When you've done something that was dangerous, then you feel fear?

MOSS Yes. I think fear is really lack of understanding of what is happening, like when you're a child you're frightened of the dark because you don't understand what's there, and if you come in to a corner and you're going what you consider is fast enough and suddenly something happens, after you've tried to sort out the mess you're in, then you get frightened.

FREEMAN Is it on the whole your natural temperament that you have to screw your courage up to take the risks or do you have to restrain your enthusiasm when you're racing?

MOSS No, I don't have to restrain and I don't have to screw my courage up. Well, no, that needs qualification. Actually I do occasionally have to screw my courage up if somebody's going very, very fast in practice and I want to go a bit quicker. To give you an example, in Syracuse there was one corner which I had never taken quite flat out, at this time about 150 miles an hour, and I was always just easing off. Well, in a racing car there is a big difference on your time – when I say a big difference, a tenth – between easing off and absolutely flat on the floor, but there's also psychologically a very big difference – in other words, you feel you're really dead safe lifting off, but if you keep your foot down you're near in trouble. And I came in to this corner and the only way I could bring myself to taking it flat out was by looking down at my instruments, not watching the road – you know, setting the car up and then looking up when it was too late to lift off. And also going on to a banked track like Monza, where you've got to get the car up at about eighty degrees, this also frightens me because of the extra possibilities of mechanical failure.

FREEMAN What about seeing crashes while you're driving – seeing other people killed? Does this disturb you?

MOSS Yes, it does. Well, always we know the driver, or practically always, except perhaps in a very big race like the Mili Milia, but in grand prix racing and most of the sports car races, you do know the drivers. And you may not know whether it's fatal or not, but to see an accident is something that is upsetting. Equally, of course, you mustn't let it worry you because if it does you become much more of a danger to yourself. I mean, it does worry you but you mustn't let it affect you, I should say.

FREEMAN Are you in fact conscious all the time that death is very close to you if you make a mistake?

MOSS No, not when I'm driving. I am when I think about it but I prefer not to. I mean, death is something which frightens me and thinking of it isn't going to make it less likely to happen, therefore I don't think about it.

FREEMAN Have you ever really thought you were done?

MOSS Yes, I have. At Monza, my steering sheared at 165 on this banked track and my arms just shot round like this and the thing was out of control and I had virtually no brakes and I remember going up, hitting the top of the wall, and closing my eyes, forcing back on the steering wheel with my feet, and then there was a whole hoohah – I don't know exactly what happened because I had my eyes closed – and the car came to a standstill. I jumped out and there was dust and everything, and I remember thinking, Well, if this is hell, you know, it's not very hot, or if it's heaven, why is it so dusty, and I was absolutely convinced that I was a goner. Actually even last week I thought that I'd had it, at Zandvoort, the tyre burst at 120 and I lost control and shot across the road because I was taking a corner and there was a big wood there and I thought, Well, this is my lot. I managed somehow to regain control in time, or the car came back – anyway, something happened and it was all right. I felt frightened while it was happening but immediately after I didn't get the feeling of fear because I had something else to think about. The tyre was burst, my second position was lost, I had to get back to the pits and so on.

FREEMAN Is this sport in fact as risky as spectators think it is or do you calculate it to the point where the risk isn't really all that great?

MOSS It is a calculated risk but there are unfortunate things which you can't calculate for, which are mechanical failures and oil on the track. I am not normally afraid of killing myself. I'm frightened of being killed by something over which I have no control.

FREEMAN Outside motor racing are you afraid of anything? Heights, for instance? Water?

MOSS No, I don't think I'm frightened of any of the normal things.

FREEMAN Not even of mice!

MOSS No, not of mice!

FREEMAN Do you believe in God?

MOSS Yes, I do. I'm not religious, though.

FREEMAN Do you ever have a thought of that kind in a moment of fear, that you want to pray or that you're near to God?

MOSS Not at that time, no, because invariably when you have an accident, or near accident, you've got so much to think about, self-preservation seems to come before everything.

FREEMAN In fact you trust yourself?

MOSS Well, yes. I trust myself but I must admit that if I think about it now I trust that God is with me and helping me. I'm religious inasmuch as I believe that there's a God. I'm not religious inasmuch as I don't believe in going to church. I had too much of it thrust down my throat when I was at school.

FREEMAN It's said of you that you're very superstitious, at least as far as your racing is concerned. Is that true?

MOSS Yes. We have in motor racing practically all superstitions which I follow. There are superstitions which go too far, such as when you see a blood-wagon – an ambulance – some people cross their fingers and count three dogs! Well, this would mean I'd have to drive all the way round the race with my fingers crossed, and it's not very practical! I feel that I have with reservations all the superstitions.

FREEMAN And do you really believe this, or is this just a kind of convention of the sport?

MOSS No, I've been brought up with it. My mother is superstitious, and I got scarlet fever and nephritis and appendicitis and everything on Friday the thirteenth, which didn't help, and I can't see any disadvantage in being superstitious, quite frankly, and therefore I accept it as just part of life.

FREEMAN I see. Yes. Well, now looking at your career what would you say is your greatest asset as a race driver?

MOSS Oh, that's a very difficult question. I think that at the moment possibly the fact that I can usually keep up a high speed over a long time. Today motor racing is more competitive than it has ever been in my career, and if you ease off a fifth of a second you may drop from first to sixth place. Two, three years ago if you eased off a fifth of a second you might drop from first to second or second to third. Therefore you've got to keep the pressure up all the time and I would say possibly this is the greatest advantage I have, I can concentrate without having to think about it.

FREEMAN How old were you when you first wanted to be a racing driver?

MOSS I think sixteen. I worked at it from the moment that I really felt I wanted to be a racing driver. My father at the beginning wouldn't let me and then ultimately he weakened – I kept on at him, you know, and water gets through a stone in the end, I suppose.

FREEMAN Was there ever any serious alternative?

MOSS Originally I was supposed to be a dentist and I'm not really that brainy, you know, I couldn't get through my exams, and so we had to throw that over, and then my father and I discussed it and we thought, Well, the hotel business was an interesting one, and I started as a trainee in that.

FREEMAN You say you couldn't get through your exams, but do you believe that?

MOSS In my own defence, I suppose I did lose two or three years of schooling through illness, from this nephritis and so on, also I just wasn't that interested in lessons and possibly I didn't pay enough attention. Another thing is that I knew quite a lot of the stuff, I think, but couldn't put it down properly, and a lot of the subjects that we had to take didn't interest me – Latin and history and so on – and so I didn't pay much attention.

FREEMAN Yes. Now, you, I believe, claim to be the first in this country of the really professional race drivers – that's true, is it?

MOSS Yes, I think so.

FREEMAN Well, now, will you tell me just what that means. What is the difference in this sport between a professional and an amateur?

MOSS The way I would like to qualify it is this. It's nothing to do with money in the normal accepted sense. The professional driver I think has to go fast whether he's got the stomach-ache or not and if he gets into a car he's expected to go faster than any other amateur's gone in that car; whether he knows the car or whether he knows the circuit or not, it doesn't really matter. You are expected always to give your best. And the other thing is that I do make practically all my income from motor racing. There are people who are professional that make some of their income from racing but are still in my mind professional inasmuch as they do it because they feel the compulsion of the sport, they really enjoy it and they feel they just want to go fast.

FREEMAN But is it true that you blazed a new trail, so that a boy without much money now, if he's got the talent, can go into motor racing successfully, whereas before your day perhaps he wouldn't have been able to?

MOSS Well, I won't say I blazed the trail, I think I've come along with it. When I started I had a very much easier road than they would today because I only had to beat a very few people, and motor racing was starting and therefore a lot of interest was focused on it, which of course it is now, but if I beat three or four people then I won. Now, somebody starting in the same position today would have to beat thirty or forty to win and these thirty or forty are very much better than I was in those days. The whole competition has come up to such a high level that a chap starting now would have a very difficult job to break into the sport.

FREEMAN How much money did you have when you started? Your father helped you, for instance?

MOSS He helped me partially. I sold my bicycle to him and I sold my radio and all sorts of odds and ends that I had – all the muck I didn't really need, you know, I passed on to my father and sort of said, 'You can have all this load of stuff if you'll let me have a racing car,' and he said, 'Well no, you can't have a racing car, you have a sports car,' and so I got a sports car. I had reasonable success –

FREEMAN When you were seventeen?

MOSS When I was seventeen, yes, and then I managed to drag my father over to a racing-car manufacturer's garage where I showed him this car, and I tried it on and he tried it on, and I think really he felt the bug because he'd done it before, and he agreed that if I sold the sports car and used the money I could buy the other one. So actually I started off originally with, say, £500, and my father helped me with £200 or £300 more.

FREEMAN Yes, so that you really started in a pretty small way and now Stirling Moss Limited is a pretty big business today?

MOSS Yes, fairly big. It's all connected with motor racing and ancillary things.

FREEMAN I wanted to ask a bit about these ancillary things. For instance, how much do you exploit your resources on the side? You sponsor some commercial products, don't you?

MOSS Yes, I sponsor fuel and oil, tyres, brake-linings, plugs – this sort of thing. I've been asked to do other things, shirts and, you know, sort of rock 'n' roll stuff practically. I haven't done that.

FREEMAN And you make yourself personally responsible for the recommendation that you give?

MOSS Yes, I do actually use anything that I recommend. I think that's important.

FREEMAN What about personal appearances? Do you make them for fees?

MOSS Sometimes for fees, sometimes not. If I give talks or lectures, which I don't like doing, and I get very little time to do, then there's no fee; if I go along and open a bazaar or something, if it's a charity there's no fee, if it isn't then there might be a fee. It really depends on what it's for.

FREEMAN What about test driving? I mean, a horse-racing jockey spends a lot of his time riding work, not on the racecourse at all. Are you doing that a lot of the time?

MOSS We do quite a lot of testing just before the race, on the circuit. Also I do a certain amount of testing during the winter. I do also write for newspapers on road tests of cars – that's when I've got a licence, of course; at the moment I'm doing bicycles, you see! If I went to a racing-car manufacturer to develop his car, then I would expect to get a fee if he was a competitor against the one I'm racing for.

FREEMAN Do you take steps to encourage fans in the same way that an actor might do?

MOSS Yes, I answer any fan mail that I get.

FREEMAN How many fan letters on an average do you get?

MOSS Well, I've never really counted. It's about 10 000 letters a year go out of the office, of which a fair proportion are fan letters.

FREEMAN And I imagine that you're very easily recognised in public places?

MOSS Sometimes too easily, yes!

FREEMAN Does this give you satisfaction on the whole, or not?

MOSS It's satisfaction if you want a table when you can't get one; it's not satisfaction if you're trying to look at an exhibition and somebody recognises you and you've got to write autographs. I think that I would miss it, but I find it embarrassing on occasions. It cuts both ways.

FREEMAN What is the size of the organisation of Stirling Moss Limited?

MOSS I have a secretary, a manager, and my father gives counsel.

FREEMAN Do you keep, for instance, an extensive card index – let's say of a particular track that you've raced on – detailed notes of where you have to brake and what the corner is like –

MOSS Not very detailed, no. Some companies that we race for ask us to fill out one and we do that, otherwise I do keep a diary every day with certain relevant facts, of what revs I got out of certain corners, if they're particularly important ones.

FREEMAN Yes. Well now, you're a pretty prosperous man now?

MOSS I suppose, yes, you'd say fairly prosperous.

FREEMAN Figures don't mean very much but do you in fact have all the money to spend that you actually want?

MOSS No, I don't.

FREEMAN Have you got very expensive tastes?

MOSS Yes, I have expensive tastes. There are quite a lot of things which I haven't got that I would like but I prefer it that way. I don't think that I'd like to have everything I want. I find certain things anyway in life rather frustrating and I think that would increase the frustration. On the other hand if they're small things, then I can buy them if necessary.

FREEMAN Do you care about money a lot?

MOSS A fair amount.

FREEMAN Do you save it against the time when you have to retire?

MOSS Yes. Yes, I do. Perhaps too much. Less now than I did a year ago.

FREEMAN When do you think you will have to retire?

MOSS I would retire if somebody passed me on a corner in a similar car – in other words if I felt that somebody was going definitely considerably faster than me and my car was right, then I would retire.

FREEMAN How long do you give yourself? You must have some notion. You're about thirty now, are you?

MOSS Yes. In years I really don't know because it is now very competitive. Physically I could most likely take it for quite a few more years. Whether mentally it's worth while doing it I don't know, but on the other hand, against that, it would be very, very difficult to give up motor racing. I don't know quite what would be a substitute for what I get out of it, the exhilaration and the excitement and the travel and all the other things.

FREEMAN Have you in fact thought whether you could live easily without it?

MOSS Well, I find it very difficult to relax. I can't go and just lay on a beach and get some sun, I would like to be spear-fishing or water-skiing or something like that. Motor racing fulfils this desire at the moment. Also I like responsibility and I have a responsibility to my mechanics, to the people I race for, and I suppose a certain amount to the public and to one's friends and family, and therefore I would want a job that would give that, and I'm not really qualified to go into any particular business, so it's going to be very, very difficult to give up racing.

FREEMAN Outside your working hours altogether, when you're enjoying your leisure, if you do enjoy it, what's your real symbol of luxury that you like spending your money on? I mean, is it a good dinner, or a luxurious flat, or taking a pretty girl out, or what is it?

MOSS Well, I like taking a pretty girl out, I like a luxurious flat as well. Funnily enough, cars don't worry me too much. I find it a little frustrating driving on the roads and therefore a car to me is much more a means of conveyance, so it isn't that side.

FREEMAN The motor-racing set are always said to live it up a great deal when they're not actually on the track, and it's difficult to reconcile that with all the physical fitness and so on that you need. Now, do you find that you can keep your nerves steady and live it up off the track?

MOSS Well, now this is a complete change round. When I started racing I was much more of a hermit and in fact right up until very recently I took it very easy for quite a few days before the race, I didn't go out and so on, and what good did it do me? I didn't get the world championship or anything else, and so I suddenly thought, Well, let's live it up a bit, and now this year, not the night before the race but up until a couple of nights before, I've been out dancing and really swinging it and having a lot of fun, and it doesn't seem to have yet affected my driving, and my personal social life is very much more fun, so until I get some proof that it's not the thing I suppose I'd like to continue doing it.

FREEMAN Is physical fitness as important as I think it probably is in this?

MOSS Very important. It's important for stamina. If you've got a half-an-hour race I think you could go and live it up all night and come out and I don't think your judgement would be impaired, but any race that lasts over half an hour or an hour, then you start to brake a few yards earlier and you put your foot down a little later and gradually you just sort of fray at the edges, and that's when it really tells.

FREEMAN How much sleep do you get in the ordinary way?

MOSS Not enough, I don't think – five, six, or seven hours – very rarely seven. I would like more but because of my late nights and early callers in the morning it seems to get less and less.

FREEMAN Do you in fact go to sleep easily or do you have to have pills?

MOSS No, I don't take pills on principle. I find that if I go to bed at twelve I'd think until three o'clock. If I go to bed at two o'clock I've got a good chance of being asleep at two or two-thirty.

FREEMAN You say you find it so difficult to relax but what do you do when you really don't want to do anything?

MOSS Oh, gosh! I never don't want to do anything. I dance, I go water-skiing, I like to go to the cinema or the theatre, I like designing, I like worrying, I suppose.

FREEMAN What do you worry about?

MOSS Oh, everything. You know, how the car's going to be, whether we've got the new gears, what I can do – I don't know, I just seem to worry, somehow. Worrying isn't really the right word, because I enjoy it, but I occupy my thoughts with things that I can really get my teeth into. I suppose mainly when I worry, it's about the car – you know – wondering whether the thing's going to last for the next race and whether other people are going to start driving faster and that sort of thing. That's the worrying I do.

FREEMAN Do you worry about not succeeding on the occasions where you don't succeed? Does this worry you?

MOSS No. What does worry me is if I think that I've driven a bad race. Whether I won it or lost it doesn't really matter. If you go out in a race, you know, you're leading or you're well positioned, and then suddenly something breaks. This is annoying, it's frustrating, but it doesn't worry me. But if I went out into a race and I drove what I felt was a bad race and won it, this would worry me mentally far more.

FREEMAN How much have you been affected by the two very heavy blows you've had recently? You've lost your wife and you've lost your British driving licence and these both happened in very quick succession. Now, did this upset you greatly?

MOSS Well, actually I had quite a few other things, troubles in business and so on, and they were all dwarfed by the trouble that I had with my wife. It did upset me very much at the time, yes, and I think that now I try to take the view that it's no good worrying about it, that my wife has a life to lead and so have I, and if I worry I think it would be very bad for my racing, which in other words is my life, and therefore I'm trying to push it to the back of my mind.

FREEMAN Well now, this leads me to ask you a very candid question indeed. Do you think you're fit to be married to anybody while you're still in active racing?

MOSS Not really. I think it's very difficult for the wife, it's very difficult for the husband, because the last thing you want is a woman around who's worrying you. Now, my wife didn't, she was very good in that way, but I think it's difficult for a woman not to, and you are conscious of the fact that she should be, and is, obviously, worried. Also I would like children and I feel that it's bad in racing to have children, because it must slow you up a bit – I *think*, anyway – and if you slow up a little bit then you drop an awful long way back and if you're a professional racing driver you are in there to try and win. If it isn't this much of your life then I think you should be at something else.

FREEMAN In other words, there's a tug here which you haven't yet resolved – I mean, could you give up racing if a woman were to say to you that she'd marry you if you gave up racing? Do you think this would be possible?

MOSS Yes, I think it would be possible, but there again I must qualify it. To give up something that is so much of your life and means so much to you – you can't say it means as much as your wife because it's so different, but something that means so much – I don't know if that would work, and equally I'm not going to say that if I continue racing and if I get involved with somebody else that I wouldn't marry them. I really don't know. I don't really think that if I had stopped racing it would have saved my marriage.

FREEMAN Have you been conscious these last few months of snide publicity in the newspapers about your domestic affairs or not?

MOSS Yes, I have. I find it very disturbing because I feel that one's private life should be, if possible, for oneself only, and it's very difficult. When I got back from seeing my wife I arrived at my flat at midnight and there were about twenty reporters there, and it's very difficult to know exactly what to do with them, whether just to say, 'Look, will you all get the hell out of here,' or whether you invite them in and try and treat them with respect, which is what I try to do.

FREEMAN These were gossip writers, they were not sporting journalists?

MOSS No, no. None of the sporting journalists actually came to me about my troubles with my wife, which I thought was very, very nice. They were all gossip writers and unfortunately gossip writers are inclined to make up things anyway, and if you say nothing they'll make up enough to make an inference, which is unfortunate, and I always believe myself – they have a job to do, the same as I do – in trying to be honest with them. But it is a very difficult problem because you feel that your private life should be your own, and where do you draw the line? They ask embarrassing questions which you can decline to answer, and I do, but nevertheless they can put an inference in by just a comma here or a word there.

FREEMAN Thinking for the moment of the loss of your driving licence, do you resent this, do you think an injustice was done, or do you think it was inevitable?

MOSS In my own mind I'm satisfied that it should not have been taken away. I feel that if my name had been John Smith it most likely wouldn't have been taken away, but there again I'm not qualified to say. I don't know enough about the courts. It obviously has been a very big blow.

FREEMAN You do realise, don't you, that you have an obligation to be a sort of public symbol of safe driving?

MOSS Yes, and I have to write about safe driving, and that is to me rather difficult. Since I haven't had a licence I've been driven by a lot of people, and I sit in the back sometimes trembling, wishing I'd got my crash-hat on, thinking, Well, this chap's got his licence and I'm sure that I'm safer on the road than this person is, who's driving me! I really mean that. What am I to do? I can't do anything about it.

FREEMAN Have you had an unfortunate reaction from your fans since this – you know, the fallen idol?

MOSS No. I would say entirely the opposite, as a matter of fact. I think that people have been very, very nice. People think it's rather amusing. I don't resent that because I can understand how they feel. It isn't amusing, but I'd far rather they felt that than, well, that's what you darn well deserve!

FREEMAN Well now, you said a minute ago that you yourself would like to have children, and I'm going to ask you a last question. Suppose in seventeen or eighteen years' time a boy of yours comes to you and says he'd like to be a racing driver, what are you going to say to him?

MOSS I would try to stop him from being a racing driver. Racing has brought me my greatest happinesses, I suppose, and quite a lot of unhappiness. I think I would try to stop him because I'm inclined to be selfish. What my mother and father have to go through must be absolute hell, and I really am very sorry that I can't find anything else that gives me what I want and yet is more unselfish towards them. I would try to stop him.

EVELYN WAUGH

INTRODUCTION

In June 1960 John Freeman's *Face to Face* interview was with the novelist and satirist Evelyn Waugh. It was Waugh's television debut and he was in an anxious frame of mind.

He seems to be making a studied attempt to appear bored, and in legendary Waugh style was obstructive, irritable and curt and even corrected Freeman whenever he could. In short Waugh gave Freeman a rough ride as an interviewer! He was most certainly antagonistic towards John Freeman. And he must surely have had in mind an episode from his novel *The Ordeal of Gilbert Pinfold.* In it Pinfold is interviewed by a man from the BBC called Angel, and detects in his questions an underlying malice – even an intrusion on his privacy. 'Pinfold', writes Waugh, 'answers succinctly and shrewdly, disconcerting his adversaries, if adversaries they were.' But the episode preys on Pinfold's mind and becomes part of his breakdown.

Waugh had had a nervous breakdown himself in 1954, and some say a searching interview with BBC Radio had contributed to it. Waugh admits to Freeman that *Pinfold* was autobiographical.

Perhaps Waugh had already rehearsed his *Face to Face* interview in his imagination and would not allow himself the possibility of a pleasant experience in reality.

Who knows? But whatever Waugh's state of mind, at the time of the interview, the brittle, sometimes cynical humour that was such a trademark of his writing, is never far from the surface.

And it's simply a delight just to observe the novelist who wrote such memorable books as, among others, *Decline and Fall, A Handful of Dust,* the *Sword of Honour* trilogy featuring Guy Crouchback and *Brideshead Revisited.*

INTERVIEW

FREEMAN Mr Waugh, I'd like to start at the very beginning of your life. Where were you born?

WAUGH I have no memory of the event. I'm told it occurred at 11 Hillfield Road, West Hampstead. I believe it's all been demolished now, like most places.

FREEMAN What's your earliest memory of a family home?

WAUGH Well, my father built a little house on a plot of land in a village called North End, Hampstead, a little hamlet – absolutely rural village within five miles of London. That's where he settled. It was quite distinct from Hampstead and had a village pub, famous in song, called the Bull and Bush, a little village shop and post office combined, it had a dairy farm and the dairyman who sold his own milk, a lady of the manor – entirely like an English rural village now.

FREEMAN Your father was a publisher, was he not?

WAUGH He was a publisher and a writer, literary critic, minor poet – he liked books and he liked writing. Man of letters, I think, would be the word for him, really.

FREEMAN Was he reasonably prosperous? I mean, how big was the house, for instance?

WAUGH Oh well – for those days, tiny. Bigger than most people live in now.

FREEMAN You've one elder brother? Do you remember him at that time?

WAUGH My memory's awfully bad. I was of course aware of his existence. He was five years older than me and always very much more advanced. I mean, by the time I was at prep school he was at public school, by the time I was at public school he was in the army and so on. So I really didn't know him at all well until, oh, after the first war.

FREEMAN If your memory's bad it's quite interesting to ask you if you've got any vivid pictorial memory of those days at that house at North End.

WAUGH I'm told that at the age of four I was taken to Hampstead

Heath Fair by my father and greatly indulged in all the coconut shies and things and that when told I must get back for luncheon I rolled on the ground and shouted, 'You brute, you beast, you hideous ass!' I was never allowed to forget that as a child but I've got no personal memory of it.

FREEMAN Do your mother and father stand equal in your memory now or is your father clearer?

WAUGH Equal, I think.

FREEMAN Were you rather strictly brought up in the Edwardian manner?

WAUGH No. No, I had an absolutely lyrically happy childhood. I think that's why I have so few memories of it. Until I went to prep school I was taught by my mother – and very well taught, I think, in the rudiments.

FREEMAN Your parents of course were not Catholics?

WAUGH Oh no.

FREEMAN Did your mother give you religious instruction?

WAUGH Yes.

FREEMAN Of a simple Anglican broad church view of the world?

WAUGH Yes. They were both pious church-going Anglicans.

FREEMAN How old were you when you could first read and write?

WAUGH I couldn't write *fluently* till I was seven.

FREEMAN Did you tell stories or even enjoy listening to stories very much when you were extremely small?

WAUGH Oh, yes, certainly. I don't think telling so much but being read to a great deal.

FREEMAN How old were you when you first wrote a story?

WAUGH I think seven, seven and a half. It was called *The Curse of the Horse Race* and it was a warning against the dangers of betting, one of the temptations to which my father was never at all subject. He was never at a racecourse in his life! I had a Calvinist nanny and I think perhaps she told me something about the dangers of horse-racing; but it's plain from the story that I didn't know anything at all about the technique of the turf.

FREEMAN Would you have liked, do you think, to be a member of a bigger family than you were?

WAUGH I'm sure the children of large families are happier in later life, but that's a different question. At that age I was clearly very happy basking in my mother's undivided attention.

FREEMAN But now, with hindsight, you realise the value of big families?

WAUGH I realise a large family's much the best, yes.

FREEMAN Had you any consciousness of missing having a sister at that age?

WAUGH I wasn't aware of missing anything. My life was idyllically happy.

FREEMAN I have noticed in one or two of your books – particularly in *Put Out More Flags* – that there's a very curious brother–sister relationship, and I wondered whether this is a problem which has exercised you a lot.

WAUGH No, you must allow the novelists their imagination to roam more freely than that, you know!

FREEMAN Well, I do. Then to school. Most of your family went to Sherborne?

WAUGH My father was absolutely miserable at Sherborne and had no memory of it except of terror and cruelty and he never went back to the school, but when it came to sending my brother to school, the first thing he did was to put him down for Sherborne!

FREEMAN Well, why didn't he put you down?

WAUGH He did put me down, indeed, but then my brother at the age of seventeen wrote a book called *The Loom of Youth*, based on his school-days, and so I was blackballed and they had hastily to find some alternative for me.

FREEMAN Which was Lancing?

WAUGH Yes. I think it was very fortunate.

FREEMAN You don't have any feeling of resentment about that?

WAUGH No. Sherborne is clearly a more beautiful little old town to grow up in. The thing about Lancing, certainly in my day, was its complete isolation. I might have been living on an island miles from anywhere. I never saw any other human life except the life of the school.

FREEMAN You have said that you were not particularly happy there.

WAUGH Have I? Whom to?

FREEMAN Well, you've been reported in public and you've never denied it, so I take it that you've said it.

WAUGH Well, I wouldn't like you to think that I was bullied or miserable or anything. The thing is, I went there in 1917 and of course all schools were beastly in 1917. One was always hungry, always cold, chilblains, the Corps taking up a great deal of one's time. But then it was rather nice because suddenly life got better and better, suddenly sweets began to appear, and cakes. All the good masters had been at the war of course, one had been taught by really rather dreary old dug-outs, and then the good young masters came back, so that one had a sensation of a gradually opening, brightening scene.

FREEMAN Were you a conformist at school?

WAUGH You mean did I obey the rules?

FREEMAN Did you obey the rules and generally toe the line of school convention?

WAUGH No, I wouldn't say that, but, you see, we were rather strictly brought up and severely punished. We had to take jolly good care we didn't play the fool in school or in chapel or on the football field or anywhere else.

FREEMAN Was the Anglican influence extremely strong in those days?

WAUGH Yes.

FREEMAN And did you at that time have any doubts about your religious faith?

WAUGH You'll think it absurd – my doubts began through reading Pope's *Essay on Man*, at the age of about sixteen, although as you know he was a Catholic. It was the first time I began to speculate at all metaphysically. Through the notes on Pope's *Essay on Man* I was turned on to Leibniz and so on, through that the general eighteenth-century enlightenment, and – not in any very sophisticated way – but I began then to question the truths of religion.

FREEMAN And did you in fact lose such faith as you had?

WAUGH Yes, indeed. I remember I and a fellow sacristan were folding up some sort of surplice or vestment or something and I revealed to him, in secret, while we were doing this, the fact that there was no God, and he was much shocked and he said, 'If you think that, you've got no business to touch this chasuble' – or whatever it was – 'and you must go and tell the chaplain.' And so I went off and told the chaplain that there wasn't a God and he wasn't the least impressed and didn't really, I think, do anything much to convince me there was. He was a very nice man!

FREEMAN Why did you choose to go to Hertford College at Oxford?

WAUGH They paid me.

FREEMAN You had an open scholarship in history? Did you subsequently remain a keen historian? You didn't get, in fact, a very distinguished degree? That's why I asked the question.

WAUGH I got a bad third, yes.

FREEMAN Why did this happen?

WAUGH Sloth.

FREEMAN What did you do at Oxford?

WAUGH Enjoyed myself. Grew up, you know.

FREEMAN Yes. How?

WAUGH Getting tight a lot of the time, entertaining, making new friends, writing silly little articles for undergraduate magazines – all that kind of thing.

FREEMAN It's said of you, and indeed one would perhaps deduce from your books, that you moved very much in what was then called the 'aesthetic set' at Oxford, which is very different, I think, from your present life. Is that true?

WAUGH Both those statements are true, yes.

FREEMAN Have you been conscious of any revulsion against that particular set of people at any stage or has this been a gradual development?

WAUGH Oh no, I'm still a pure aesthete! But in middle life one doesn't have to dress up in special clothes in order to enjoy architecture, you know.

FREEMAN When you were an undergraduate did you have enough money?

WAUGH I was deeply in debt, of course. We always were.

FREEMAN But you were not resentful or conscious of not having enough money? Your father gave you what you basically needed?

WAUGH He gave me more than I basically needed and I spent about twice as much.

FREEMAN When you came down from Oxford did you have to earn a living at once?

WAUGH Not at once. It was gradually borne in on me. I always wanted to be a painter and I went to an art school for a time.

FREEMAN But then your father was paying for you?

WAUGH Oh yes, and then of course the bills were beginning to come in and eventually there was a kind of debt settlement in which I revealed the state of my indebtedness. It wouldn't seem very much now but it was quite a lot then, four or five hundred pounds, I think. And so he paid them on condition I earned my living, and I went as a prep school master which was the sort of resort for the criminal classes of those days.

FREEMAN And out of which presumably *Decline and Fall* eventually emerged?

WAUGH Well, very remotely.

FREEMAN Yes. Was *Decline and Fall* a financial success?

WAUGH Still is.

FREEMAN Yes, but was it at that time?

WAUGH Not in the sense that I was immediately rich. It brought in some money.

FREEMAN How old were you when you were first conscious that you could earn a decent living by writing?

WAUGH I should think twenty-five. My memory is awfully bad for dates. I wrote a book on Rossetti when I was, I suppose, twenty-three, and then this novel, which had a sort of *succès d'estime*, brought in commissions for articles and things –

FREEMAN Yes, quite – quite. Now, how old were you when you were converted to the Catholic faith?

WAUGH I think thirty. Or just rising thirty.

FREEMAN Had you studied for a long time before your conversion?

WAUGH I was under instruction – literally under instruction – for about three months, but of course I'd interested myself in it before, reading books independently and so on.

FREEMAN Did you have a sudden revelation which led you to conversion or was it a very gradual process?

WAUGH Well, I think I'd always – that is to say, always from the age of sixteen or so – realised that Catholicism was Christianity, that all other forms of Christianity were only good so far as they chipped little bits off the main block. It was a conversion to Christianity rather than a conversion to Catholicism as such.

FREEMAN Well, this is the point I wanted to bring out. This came after a period when you had lost your faith and you regained it in the Catholic Church. You hadn't been continuously a devout and practising Christian who went over to Rome?

WAUGH Oh no. Oh no, no, no. I should think from the age of sixteen to the age of twenty-eight I didn't go to church at all, as far as I remember.

FREEMAN Since you were received into the Catholic Church have you ever seriously doubted? Never been through a period when things have been difficult for you?

WAUGH Oh, it's very *difficult* – exasperation at the extraordinary behaviour of individual clergymen –

FREEMAN Ah yes, but you've never doubted the central canon of your faith?

WAUGH Never had any doubts, no, no.

FREEMAN Looking back now, what would you say is the greatest gift in terms of tranquillity or peace of mind or whatever that your faith has given you?

WAUGH Well, it isn't a sort of lucky dip which you get something out of, you know. It's hard without using pietistic language to explain, but it's simply admitting the existence of God or dependence on God – your contact with God – the fact that everything in the world that's good depends on him. It isn't a sort of added amenity of the welfare state, that you say, Well, to all this, having made a good income, now I'll have a little icing on top, of religion. It's the essence of the whole thing.

FREEMAN You say 'all that is good in the world' comes from God. You don't seem to find very much which is good in the modern world. You've seen it consistently as a decadent world, have you not?

WAUGH But there's good in a decadent world.

FREEMAN Yes, but your purpose in life is – what? – to castigate or to chronicle the decadent world. Are you trying to scourge us into reform?

WAUGH Oh no, no, no, no, no. No, I'm just trying to write books.

FREEMAN Yes, but none the less no one who is as intellectually coherent as you are can write books, even just as finished, polished objects, without having a certain purpose in mind, I suspect.

WAUGH Quite unconscious. It wouldn't occur to me to sit down and say I will now write a book to reveal the horrors of the gangs in this district or something like that.

FREEMAN No, no. I'm sure of that. But now for instance recently you said that in your next book you're going to deal with Crouchback's realisation that no good comes from public causes but only private causes of the spirit. Now, this seems to me to be a didactic theme which the novelist is perfectly entitled to take, and I wonder when that first came to you?

WAUGH Oh, I think always. I've never believed in public causes.

FREEMAN But, you see, in your earlier books I would have said the characterisation was perhaps not profound enough to reveal the private causes of the spirit.

WAUGH No, that's quite true, but you certainly wouldn't say they revealed any public causes, would you?

FREEMAN No! No, I wouldn't indeed! What is your favourite book?

WAUGH One called *Helena* no one's ever read, but awfully good. It's the best written, the most interesting theme.

FREEMAN What in particular fascinated you about Helena? She's an unusual saint.

WAUGH Yes, that's one of the fascinating things, you see. Practically nothing's known about her.

FREEMAN Catholicism in your books does seem very much to be equated with the aristocratic life and so on. I wonder, would you be equally interested in writing a book about the Little Flower, some Irish peasant saint, for instance, or a really humble –

WAUGH But it wasn't about her sanctity I was writing, it was about the conditions of fourth-century Rome, you see. She happened to be the empress. It wasn't the fact of her rank that made her interesting, it was the fact of her finding the true cross made her interesting.

FREEMAN Is humility –

WAUGH If I might continue, the fact of the true cross was that there was an actual piece of wood, a historical fact, behind the gospel.

Whether or not the wood she found was the cross is open to doubt, but at that time all those Asiatic cults, the Gnostics and people, were trying to theorise and symbolise and fine away the simple facts of an actual crucifixion on a piece of wood, and she I represented as being a simple English girl thrown to her disgust into the imperial life, not the least enjoying the high position, and putting her finger at once on what was wrong with Imperial Rome at that time: which was, they were losing the sense of actuality. That, you might indeed say, was a didactic book.

FREEMAN Could I ask you some questions now about *Pinfold*? The question that everybody broadly wants to ask you is how far *Pinfold* is an account of your own brief illness?

WAUGH Almost exact. In fact, it had to be cut down a lot. It would be infinitely tedious to have recorded everything. It's the account of three weeks' hallucinations going on absolutely continuously.

FREEMAN And you heard voices?

WAUGH I heard all these voices. If I'd written down everything the voices said, it would have been immensely boring. One had to be selective.

FREEMAN But did they say the same thing to you that they said to Pinfold?

WAUGH Oh yes, rather. Again and again and again, day and night.

FREEMAN And there were three different kinds of voices really who talked to Pinfold; there was the beautiful girl who made appointments with him –

WAUGH They gradually thinned down, if you remember the book. At first I conceived that everyone was involved – I was rationalising it all the time, it was not in the least like losing one's reason, it was simply one's reason working hard on the wrong premisses.

FREEMAN Yes. But I wonder why the voices said what they did? I mean, have you any notion –

WAUGH I always wondered that.

FREEMAN – why you should conjure up this lovely girl who made appointments, and you never kept the appointment?

WAUGH Half did, if you remember the story – went out to look for her and she wasn't there.

FREEMAN And then the other, the most odious voice said that Pinfold was a homosexual, a communist Jew, a parvenu and so on. Were these the kind of hallucinations that you yourself felt?

WAUGH Oh yes, those were the voices exactly.

FREEMAN And in your own life was it the neighbours who were making these remarks, because if you remember in *Pinfold* his neighbours were involved in this persecution.

WAUGH I've no idea what my neighbours said about me!

FREEMAN But did you feel that your neighbours were –

WAUGH No. The whole thing was so puzzling I had to, if you remember, invent the theory that the Broadcasting Society – your own people – were involved.

FREEMAN Well, I was going to ask you. Have you in fact a particular deep feeling about the BBC? It comes again into a number of your books, which is why I asked, always in a slightly pejorative context.

WAUGH Well, everyone thinks ill of the BBC, but I don't think I'm more violent than anybody else.

FREEMAN In the life that you've chosen to lead now – the life of a country gentleman, almost a squirearchic life – do you get on happily with your neighbours?

WAUGH Well, it's not really accurate to say I lead a squirearchic life, sitting on the bench of magistrates and going round cattle shows and that kind of thing. I lead a life of absolute solitude.

FREEMAN You don't, in fact, take part in the activities of your –

WAUGH No. I live in the country because I like to be alone.

FREEMAN Well now, you have made a very noticeable rejection of life, because at one time you lived in the town, you mixed in society, you wrote books about society, and now you've withdrawn completely. Were you conscious of a sudden decision to do that?

WAUGH It happened about eight years ago, not suddenly but I gradually got bored with society, largely I think through deafness – I can hear one person perfectly, but if there's a crowd I get dazed; but I think it's probably psychosomatic because I don't hear because I'm bored, not I'm bored because I can't hear.

FREEMAN Do you ever reflect on the difference between the sort of life you've chosen now and your own family background?

WAUGH There's very little difference.

FREEMAN One wonders – this may sound rude but it genuinely arises out of the things you've said and the things you've written – one wonders whether this is in some curious way a kind of charade, that you've decided to assume the attitude of country life, which in your books doesn't seem as if it's entirely natural to you.

WAUGH It's quite true I haven't the smallest interest in country life, in the agricultural sense or the local government sense. The country to me is a place where I can be silent.

FREEMAN Are you very sensitive to the criticisms of others – unkind reviews of your books?

WAUGH I don't think so.

FREEMAN I've often wondered, for instance, at the time in the middle of the thirties when you were assailed by – well, by Rose Macaulay and one or two others for being a fascist, because you reported the Abyssinian war from the Italian side – did that upset you or prey on your mind at all?

WAUGH I wasn't even aware she assailed me.

FREEMAN Well then, that's a very effective answer! Have you ever brooded on what appears to you to be unjust or adverse criticism?

WAUGH No, I'm afraid if someone praises me I think what an ass and if they abuse me I think what an ass.

FREEMAN And if they say nothing about you at all and take no notice of you?

WAUGH That's the best I can hope for.

FREEMAN Why are you appearing in this programme?

WAUGH Poverty. We've both been hired to talk in this deliriously happy way.

FREEMAN Now, you constantly tell people that you're poor and I don't want to ask you impertinent questions, but you're a great deal luckier than many people because you made something of a fortune before the war, before it was all taxed away.

WAUGH Never saved a penny. And of course no honest man has been able to save any money in the last twenty years.

FREEMAN Looking at yourself, as I'm sure you are a self-critical person, what do you feel is your worst fault?

WAUGH Irritability.

FREEMAN Are you a snob at all?

WAUGH I don't think so.

FREEMAN Irritability with your family, with strangers?

WAUGH Absolutely everything. Inanimate objects and people, animals, anything.

FREEMAN May I put a Catholic question to you out of the penny catechism. Do you remember the twelve fruits of the Holy Ghost?

WAUGH I should do, I don't.

FREEMAN Well, they include charity, joy, patience, benignity, mildness – do you fall short in these?

WAUGH Yes.

FREEMAN Are you ever rude to people – nuns and priests and people in your own faith – or is this a thing you reserve rather for outsiders?

WAUGH I was never rude to a nun, obviously. I don't think I've ever been rude to a priest, no. That's more respect for authority and not –

FREEMAN It's not a feeling of oneness, it's not being on the inside with him? Do you feel the need to belong to an organisation all the time?

WAUGH The best I can tell you in that way is that I'm much more at ease with fellow Catholics than I am with heathens or Protestants. One has so many basic assumptions in common that there's so much doesn't need saying, and when you're talking to even the most amusing and intelligent heathen you suddenly find that something you've said has no meaning at all to him.

FREEMAN How high in your scale of virtues do you put the Christian duty of service to others?

WAUGH It isn't for me to make these scales. My service is simply to bring up one family.

FREEMAN One would think from reading, for instance, the end of *Brideshead* that you attach a tremendous importance to the abnegation of self and the performing of menial tasks even. Now, is that an illusion? Do you not attach much importance to this aspect of Christian virtue?

WAUGH Oh, of course, enormous importance for the people of ascetic temperament. We aren't all called to be ascetics.

FREEMAN I'd like now to ask you a last question and I want to go back to *Pinfold*. Looking back on that mental breakdown that you had then, and then your life as you see it, can you see any permanent conflict or instability perhaps between the way of life in which you were brought up and the way of life in which you've chosen to live now?

WAUGH Oh, I know what you're getting at, that ass Priestley said that in an article.

FREEMAN Well, I was not particularly thinking of this but I was asking you whether you ever had any fear that that sort of thing may happen to you again?

WAUGH No, no. That's poor old Priestley thought that.

GILBERT HARDING

INTRODUCTION

This *Face to Face* is one of the best-known, most talked-about interviews in television's history. When it was transmitted in September 1960 it caused a sensation, and since then it seems to have passed into folk memory, half remembered even by those who never saw it. It was with Gilbert Harding.

Gilbert Harding held a reputation in the fifties and sixties which today seems out of all proportion to his talents. He came to fame as a chairman and panellist on radio and television game shows: *Round Britain Quiz*, *Twenty Questions* and *What's My Line?* But his reputation sprang not from his role, but what he made of it. People appearing on television in the fifties were far more polite, more respectful than today. Gilbert Harding was not. He was brusque, frequently rude to his guests, openly bad-tempered and once unashamedly drunk on the air. The public loved it, enjoying the outrage while deploring the rudeness, and Harding commanded an audience of 11 million.

Freeman came from a more rigorous tradition of broadcasting and, perhaps sensing something of the bully in Harding's personality, embarked on a searching interrogation. Here, perhaps more than in any of the other programmes, he seems to adopt a line of questioning more suitable for a psychoanalyst. But his approach isn't as sympathetic or as sensitive as it might have been, and he repeatedly grills Harding on questions of discipline, pain, punishment and domination. Finally Freeman probes too far, Harding becoming tearful at the memory of his dying mother. Freeman was unaware that she had died, and later admitted, 'I cannot remember any other question in the *Face to Face* programmes that I have so much regretted asking.' In fact, Harding saw the programme before transmission and not only approved the interview as fair but even defended Freeman from those who criticised him as a cruel interrogator.

Yet in the days that followed there was a great tide of sympathy for Harding. Offers of friendship poured in. Suddenly people saw him no longer as the crusty, bad-tempered performer of the quiz shows, but as lonely, sad and unhappy. Just eight weeks later, Gilbert Harding died suddenly on the steps of the BBC studios in London where he had been recording *Round Britain Quiz*. The sense of loss and regret felt by the public owed much to this *Face to Face* with John Freeman.

INTERVIEW

FREEMAN Gilbert Harding, you were brought up in the surroundings of a workhouse and then at an orphanage school, and you went to Cambridge, and you've been a schoolmaster, a policeman, a registrar's clerk, a broadcaster and a journalist. Now, at the age of only fifty-three, you're a sort of national oracle with a reputation for impatience, rudeness and occasional rather unexpected flashes of charm and good nature. Now, have you at last found a way of life which makes you happy and gives you fulfilment?

HARDING No.

FREEMAN What's lacking?

HARDING Oh, I think that the thing that is really lacking is a sense of purpose, you know.

FREEMAN Well, why do you do it?

HARDING Well, it keeps one out of the workhouse, you know; it gives one a sort of *modus vivendi*, which is a pompous way of saying a means of earning one's living, rather more than one deserves, certainly not more than one desires, and I suppose in a way it's due to a fundamental laziness.

FREEMAN One can't help reading of the record of what you've done and feeling that here perhaps is someone with a first-class mind, or at any rate a very good mind, doing work which is mostly rather below your capacity – panel games, disc jockeying and so on.

HARDING I am myself very much aware of the danger of the reputation of having a first-class mind. I've acquired a reputation for being a man of great knowledge and information whereas in fact I'm a man of what used to be in my day ordinary education, which nowadays of course would pass for a very superior education, because nowadays most people, I think, tend to get more and more illiterate.

FREEMAN Do you ever feel that you're doing work which is below your capacity?

HARDING In my more conceited moments I think I could do something more useful and more contributive, yes.

FREEMAN Have you ever thought what that might be?

HARDING Well, the thing I do better than anything else is teach. I was a very good schoolmaster, a very good teacher, but I couldn't go into that again now, could I? You see, nobody would employ me. I shouldn't be able to live on the salary, either.

FREEMAN Before we go on with that just tell me a little bit about your present life of fame and public popularity and so on. Do you enjoy, for instance, getting letters from fans?

HARDING Not really. I don't really enjoy it. I'm often touched by them but I can't write and tell everybody who writes and tells me they think that I'm wonderful, good, gracious, intelligent, brilliant and gifted, I can't bother to write and tell them that I'm nothing of the kind. I answer them generally by a courteous signed postcard saying 'Thank you for your kind and generous letter. I wish I thought as much of me as you do' or something of that sort.

FREEMAN Are you ever conscious of cultivating the mannerisms of Harding the public figure?

HARDING I've never cultivated any mannerisms. I've never pretended. If I knew how to pretend I would, but I don't know how, so I don't.

FREEMAN Well now, you tell me, slightly disappointingly perhaps, that on the whole you're not satisfied, that you're not really fulfilled in your life yet.

HARDING No, not at all satisfied.

FREEMAN All right. Looking back, are you conscious of any point where there was certainly a failure of ambition, or a mistake, or just a disappointment about your career?

HARDING I suppose if I'd worked harder at Cambridge I'd have got a better degree and therefore I could have been a schoolmaster in better schools, schools where one wasn't sort of harried and pushed about. I was in private schools which on the whole are pretty nasty. And then if it hadn't been for the war, on which so many people blamed so many things, I might have been called to the Bar. I think I might have made quite a good barrister. And I suppose if I hadn't been ill by the time I began to earn quite a lot of money, too ill to overcome a natural laziness, I might have written a good novel. I've still got about eight chapters written. But nothing has ever happened that has given me any sort of sense of achievement or satisfaction.

FREEMAN Tell me what went wrong with schoolmastering? You've just said you were pushed around, but was there more to it than that?

HARDING No, except that I didn't care very much for proprietary headmasters and so on, and I always felt very sorry for the little boys and still sorrier for their parents who were called upon to pay large fees for very little.

FREEMAN Did you ever have a real vocation for teaching or was this drifting into a job?

HARDING I drifted into it when I became a papist. There was nothing else to do.

FREEMAN Do you think you've got the patience for teaching? Because after all your public reputation is of an impatient man.

HARDING It's not altogether deserved, that reputation. I've got a great deal of patience with people who want to learn and therefore I was much more successful as a crammer – as a tutor – of grown-up people than as a sort of hired hack to teach little boys things they didn't particularly want to know.

FREEMAN Were you a good disciplinarian teaching the little boys?

HARDING Yes, I terrified them.

FREEMAN Why did you become a policeman?

HARDING Because I was fed up with being a schoolmaster and it seemed to me to be an escape. I thought that with a Cambridge degree, however squalid, shabby, third-class, I thought I might become an education officer or something, or even become a detective, and that would have been very nice, but then I broke my knee, I had a cartilage disturbance, and that was inconvenient and troublesome and in the middle of all that I was offered a job in Cyprus, so I went.

FREEMAN When you actually became a policeman did you have a dream of being a detective?

HARDING No, I had a dream of not being a schoolmaster any more and I thought that I wouldn't be a PC on the beat for all that time, and then I thought I might become promoted and important. I should have liked –

FREEMAN Yes, but there are after all a number of alternatives to schoolmastering apart from being a policeman in Bradford and I'm anxious to know why you chose this really somewhat improbable line.

HARDING Well, I used to have no money in the holidays and to keep myself amused and interested by going to the quarter sessions and assizes and the police court, and then I knew very well an important policeman in Bradford; he said, 'You look very fed up', I said, 'I am fed up', he said, 'Well, why don't you become a policeman?' I said, 'Not a bad idea,' and so I did. I became a policeman. Not very willingly or enthusiastically.

FREEMAN Did you in fact like the routine of life in the force?

HARDING I didn't really, because when I was a recruit I had to do a lot of hopping about, vaulting over horses and things like that, and keeping fit, which I've always disliked very much, and then I was on that awful shift which begins at six o'clock in the evening and ends at two o'clock in the morning and wasn't very amusing, going round and seeing whether people had locked up their premises or not. It wasn't exciting.

FREEMAN Did you ever actually arrest anybody?

HARDING Oh never. I helped once to arrest a drunk but that's all.

FREEMAN Did you get on with your colleagues in the police force?

HARDING Most of them, yes, most of them.

FREEMAN Did you like wearing the uniform?

HARDING I didn't, no. I didn't like the helmet. That's why I was hoping to get into the motor squad where I could have worn a flat cap.

FREEMAN On the whole, do you like life in big institutions? You've been a teacher in a number of schools, you've been in the BBC, you've been in the police force. One wonders if you haven't a trend in that direction.

HARDING Yes, I think I do like life in big institutions. I've often thought I'd like to join a monastery, but then I'd have to behave myself much more than I'm able to do. I think I'm happier when I'm with a lot of other people.

FREEMAN What about being in a position of administering discipline? Because again, you see, you've tended in that direction.

HARDING To *administer* discipline?

FREEMAN Indeed yes. Schoolmaster, policeman, even the holy terror of broadcasting has got a certain flavour of discipline about it.

HARDING Oh, I never thought of administering it! I'm always rather afraid of being subject to it.

FREEMAN But is it not true that being a schoolmaster, being a policeman, being a quizmaster, has got a slight cachet of discipline about it?

HARDING I never thought about that. I suppose you mean do I like bossing other people about?

FREEMAN Yes, indeed I do!

HARDING I suppose I do really.

FREEMAN If you've never done it before, I ask you now to look in on yourself and tell me if you're at all conscious of having obsessive thoughts about discipline and punishment and so on.

HARDING Do you mean in the wide sense or personally?

FREEMAN Well, in the wide sense.

HARDING I think in the wide sense I want people to know when they're wrong and to admit it. I don't think there's much point in punishing them afterwards.

FREEMAN As regards, for instance, pain – are you good at enduring pain yourself?

HARDING No, I shouldn't think I am. I do all I can to avoid it.

FREEMAN Do you fear it, in fact? Does this occur to you from time to time?

HARDING I think about it every now and then when I read about it. When I read about it I find it rather frightening.

FREEMAN What about pain in others – I mean, I don't suppose you want to inflict it, but if you see it do you shrink from it or can you stay with other people who are suffering pain?

HARDING I can stay with them if they're suffering pain but I loathe the idea of state infliction or anything of that sort. I dislike it very much.

FREEMAN The notion of the all-powerful authority upsets you?

HARDING Yes. The anonymous indeterminate authority which directs that people should be punished is awful. Any kind of torture makes me feel quite ill.

FREEMAN Well, what about the more immediately personal and passionate aspect of this? I mean, do you ever wish pain for your enemies?

HARDING No.

FREEMAN Do you have enemies? I'm sure you do.

HARDING I must have a few. I'm not aware of many. There are only two or three people in the world I dislike, and I think I've on the whole got more friends than enemies.

FREEMAN Do you ever fantasy some kind of punishment or trouble for your enemies?

HARDING No. Except occasionally if I dislike two people very much I feel it would serve them right to be alone together for a long time and have to put up with one another's conversation.

FREEMAN Could you tell me what constitutes an enemy? You said there are very few people you dislike. What is it which identifies enmity or dislike in these cases?

HARDING I dislike pomposity and pretence and, being on the whole rather selfish and jealous, I suppose – people who I think are not as intelligent as I am, I resent their success, especially when they become important and knighted and so on.

FREEMAN Do you feel very strongly yourself the need for success?

HARDING I've never consciously striven for it, but once I was aware I had it I must say that I'm terrified of losing it.

FREEMAN Are you very cautious, for instance, of tackling jobs where you're not too certain that you'll be able to do them successfully?

HARDING Very cautious indeed. Yes. I wouldn't like nowadays, at my advanced age and with all the sensitivities and miseries that have come upon me, I wouldn't like to be shown up, for instance.

FREEMAN Has this diffidence or fear ever affected the course of your career at any stage?

HARDING Yes, I put it down myself to a sort of lack of courage. I've no real courage; I shouldn't care to accept a challenge to do anything which I felt I might not do well.

FREEMAN Do you, in ordinary life, dream a lot?

HARDING I dream constantly, yes.

FREEMAN Are you apt to be the dominant figure?

HARDING No, on the whole I'm the sort of – suffering.

FREEMAN Do you dream about your work?

HARDING No, I dream about unpleasant situations and my dreams are that I didn't get out of them and they developed horribly.

FREEMAN Are you conscious that this is at all an oppressive factor in your life?

HARDING No, I'm aware of no particular oppressive factor.

FREEMAN Have you ever been with a person dying?

HARDING Yes, only once.

FREEMAN Do you remember that? Someone very close to you? Did it make a vivid impression?

HARDING It did, yes, yes.

FREEMAN Is that the only time you've seen a person dead?

HARDING Only once, yes.

FREEMAN Yes. Let's go right back to your childhood. Were you, in this rather unpromising background of first of all the workhouse and your grandfather and so on, and then the orphanage school in Wolverhampton – were you subjected to pretty stern discipline most of that time?

HARDING Yes, I suppose so. Not at home, not at the workhouse, but at the orphanage, yes.

FREEMAN Corporal punishment?

HARDING Yes.

FREEMAN Only when you went to school, or did you ever have that at home too?

HARDING Never at home, never at home, no.

FREEMAN What are your memories of that?

HARDING Oh, sort of indignation and annoyance rather than anything else.

FREEMAN Do you still remember the pain of it?

HARDING No. Nor do I have any ill will or resentment about it.

FREEMAN You didn't like your grandfather, I think?

HARDING I didn't very much, no.

FREEMAN Was he too strong a disciplinarian? What was wrong with him?

HARDING I think he and I were very much alike, now I look back on it. I think we were both rather self-satisfied, pompous and assertive, and he probably detected in me the things which he probably wasn't aware of in himself.

FREEMAN Now, was your mother, who is still alive –

HARDING She's not. She's dead.

FREEMAN I beg your pardon. Was your mother a refuge from stern discipline?

HARDING Yes, she was always a sort of comforting and on the whole rather over-ready source of assuagement and – always a sort of bosom to cry on.

FREEMAN And your sister too?

HARDING I didn't like her very much. She's dead, too. I didn't get on with her very well.

FREEMAN Looking back on your childhood, is your relation with your mother the sharpest memory that you have?

HARDING Yes.

FREEMAN Have you now, as we talk, a very clear *visual* memory of your mother, now at this instant?

HARDING A sort of patient smile and resigned shrugging of shoulders, as much as to say, Well, I shall never understand you but I suppose you know what you're doing – a rather tired and weary woman.

FREEMAN How old were you when that memory relates?

HARDING I suppose just about when I was going to Cambridge, when she was afraid I should mix with people who were above my station and waste my money and waste my time – and she was right.

FREEMAN Any vivid memory of extreme childhood, of a sudden punishment or a sudden laugh?

HARDING No. I remember throwing things about and creating scenes and tearing things up and smashing plates and pretending to be ill when I wasn't and making my temperature go up and attracting sympathy and things of that sort, which after a time she got, as they say in America, wise to, and that didn't work any more. So I had to think of something else.

FREEMAN Is there any truth in the notion I have in the back of my mind that it is this particularly deep relationship that you obviously had with your mother which has made it impossible so far for you to marry?

HARDING Yes, I think so. You see, my sister didn't marry and I didn't marry and my mother was a widow when she was thirty, and so when we came to live together we put up a sort of cloud of sexual frustration that was enough to blot out the sun, and I've never been particularly affectionate; one of my troubles is that I don't attract affection very much and when I do I tend to repel it. I'm not an intimate or cosy person. I don't really like living in close contact with anybody. I think I'm pretty difficult to live with.

FREEMAN Are you lonely as a result of this?

HARDING Profoundly lonely, yes.

FREEMAN So that if you could have worked this out, this would have been a great thing in your life?

HARDING It would have been very much better, yes. I'm often very envious of people, especially people who've got children. But I think on the whole it's better that I didn't marry.

FREEMAN Am I right in thinking that women tend to make you testy and impatient and bring out the worst side of you?

HARDING Yes, except the women I like very much, who always seem to be married to other people, and they have an assurance and a maturity which I envy. I find it very difficult to talk to most women.

FREEMAN Is fear an emotion which you're conscious of, greatly?

HARDING Yes. I think fear of illness and fear of physical loss of mobility, fear of failure – yes, I'm full of fears.

FREEMAN Those are all fears of the future. What about, for instance, fear of stepping outside your own personal little world that you've created for yourself?

HARDING Well, I'm not afraid of that, but I avoid it as I'm happier by myself. I've become a television addict and I read a great deal and I find myself either overwhelming in conversation, which afterwards I regret and think I've talked too much, or, what is even worse, I find that other people have done all the talking in which case I've been appallingly bored; so I think I'd rather stay by myself.

FREEMAN Are you afraid ever of death?

HARDING I'm not afraid of death. I'm afraid of dying. I should be very glad to be dead, but I don't look forward to the actual process of dying.

FREEMAN You've been seriously, even gravely, ill once or twice. Have you ever thought that perhaps you were going to die?

HARDING No, when one's very ill I find that one doesn't think of that. Afterwards, when people tell you how ill you've been, in my case at least, I feel why on earth did they bother. It would have been very much better to have let me go. That of course is very mean; I should feel very grateful to them.

FREEMAN But in fact you're not bothered at the thought of being dead if you could get over the hurdle of dying –

HARDING I'd much rather be dead than alive if I hadn't got to go through the miseries of actually dying.

FREEMAN But of course you have more to go through than that. I mean, are the concepts of purgatory and hell real ones to you?

HARDING I've no fear of hell, and purgatory won't be all that bad.

FREEMAN Do you have a sort of vision of what it may be like? Is it real to you?

HARDING No, except it'll be a state of cleansing, getting rid of the miseries and the stains of this world and getting ready for the next. I'm not afraid of that.

FREEMAN Is your religion a daily and active force in your life?

HARDING Ah, difficult – it's a *daily* force. It's not as active as it should be.

FREEMAN Do you find that going, for instance, to the confessional is something you do just as a duty or is it something which gives you real mental relief and satisfaction?

HARDING It gives relief and satisfaction and refreshment.

FREEMAN Have you ever been psychoanalysed?

HARDING I've started it once or twice but never gone on with it.

FREEMAN I take it at any rate that you haven't got any prejudice against it?

HARDING I'm sure that psychiatrists are able to help lots of people but I think they have to be ready to be helped and willing and pliant, and I'm not very willing and not very pliant and not very convinced. Therefore I think it's on the whole a waste of their time and of mine.

FREEMAN And yet I take it from the fact that you've started it once or twice that you would in some way like to change yourself?

HARDING Yes, I've felt the need for it. I'd like somebody to tell me how to behave better, but after all I know, and the best psychoanalysts really are priests.

FREEMAN Is that the greatest blessing that your conversion to the Roman Catholic faith has brought you – the ability to confess and to have this close relation with the priest?

HARDING Yes, I think that is the greatest sort of logical, cool guidance in the heat and burden of the day.

FREEMAN Your bad behaviour consists mainly in occasional explosive bad temper – sometimes to people who aren't very good at standing up for themselves. Now, can you look into your own heart and tell us why it is that you're a victim to this particular weakness?

HARDING I suppose it's bad manners and bad temper. It's quite indefensible but I'm never willingly rude to people who as you say can't answer back or can't stand up – never willingly – I quite often am, I suppose, by accident. I'm always very sorry and say so. But I quite often lose my temper and am very rude to people who are in a much better position to answer back, and they often do.

FREEMAN What qualities in life, which experience tells you are essential to happiness, are the ones that you most feel you lack?

HARDING Companionship, security and a sense of purpose.

FREEMAN Tell me for what blessing in your life you'd really most wish to thank your family or your friends or even the world in general.

HARDING I suppose I was born with a good memory and after having stammered very badly until I was eleven, since then I've had what is vulgarly called 'the gift of the gab'.

LORD REITH

INTRODUCTION

The year 1989 is the centenary of the birth of the first Director-General of the BBC: Lord Reith, whose 'face to face' with John Freeman was first shown in October 1960. His ideals, of a BBC independent of political and commercial pressures, are still ideals followed to this day.

Although he had been retired from the BBC for over twenty years, Lord Reith was renowned as the head of a broadcasting monopoly and the man who decided everything the nation should see on television and hear on radio. Lord Reith introduced many familiar features of today's broadcasting: educational and political programmes, the *Radio Times*, weather forecasts and the Greenwich pips; and the prestigious Reith Lectures, named in his honour, continue to this day.

In 1938, after sixteen years, Reith left the BBC to become chairman of Imperial Airways, later BOAC. During the war he was successively Minister for Information, for Transport, for Works and Planning, and at the time of this interview had held high office in a number of corporations and companies. Yet none of these achievements seems to have given him the kind of satisfaction he had experienced as the Director-General.

'John Charles Walsham Reith, late BBC and regrets he ever left it' was his entry in the visitors' book when he appeared on *Face to Face*. He was seventy-one, and it was his first television appearance. The viewers enjoyed being able to watch this 'terrifying personality' from a safe distance. Yet John Freeman, in a recent interview, recalled finding in him 'an almost pathetic desire to be liked and supported by other people':

> Certainly one can't help feeling sympathy for Reith who admits in this interview he had not had a happy life. He was to live another eleven years.
>
> At a time of such impending changes in broadcasting, it's fitting to look back at probably the most influential man in television history.

INTERVIEW

FREEMAN Lord Reith, when you became General Manager of the British Broadcasting Company, in 1922, the company virtually didn't exist. When you resigned from being Director-General of the BBC in 1938, I suppose it was the most influential non-government organisation in the world. Now, did you foresee any of that when you first wrote your letter of application in 1922?

REITH Not then – I literally didn't know what broadcasting was. The advertisement was attractive, I thought it was the sort of thing I wanted, and I applied.

FREEMAN Can you remember what you said in your letter of application, because it must have been a very ingenious one, if you got the job without knowing what it was?

REITH I addressed an application, posted it in the club letter-box – Cavendish Club in Piccadilly; then I did what I ought to have done before posting the letter, I went to look up the man in *Who's Who* and I retrieved my letter from the club box, which took some doing. Rewrote the letter, with a reference to my Aberdonian ancestry, and that, I think, at least ensured that I was on the short list.

FREEMAN And did you really have qualifications at that time for this job, do you think?

REITH Oh, I had qualifications for managing, I thought, almost anything. That all right?

FREEMAN Fine, yes. Well now, I'd like to take you back and put you, as far as possible, in your natural setting. You're the youngest son of a Free Church minister in Glasgow, is that right?

REITH We don't like being called Free Church – it's the established Church of Scotland.

FREEMAN You were comfortably off in your childhood?

REITH Relatively.

FREEMAN How many brothers and sisters?

REITH Four of one and two of the other. The nearest to my age was ten years older than I.

FREEMAN So you were really brought up as a lonely child?

REITH Yes.

FREEMAN Were you conscious of religion in your family life?

REITH Yes, perhaps more conscious of that than anything else.

FREEMAN In what sort of form? For instance, family prayers with full ceremony?

REITH Indeed – morning and night.

FREEMAN And how often did you have to go to church?

REITH Every Sunday twice, and Sunday school as well. And when I got older the Wednesday evening prayer meetings. I liked to go. I enormously admired my father's preaching, and the music was very good. I enjoyed it.

FREEMAN Did you take what your father told you about religion without question, or did you ever doubt?

REITH I don't think I doubted, not in the early years. I certainly never expressed any doubts to him. I don't think that I ever had – nor yet have – doubts about fundamentals. One sat more easily to certain points of dogma and doctrine as one got older, but as to fundamentals, no change.

FREEMAN And that maintains to this day?

REITH I believe profoundly but practise poorly.

FREEMAN Did you take everything that your father told you on trust, or only religion?

REITH I accepted a good deal of other things without agreeing with them.

FREEMAN Did you have a close relation with your father?

REITH Not until I was thirty, and he was seventy-five.

FREEMAN Most people, at any rate in the south of England, would suppose that life in a manse in Glasgow was austere, not very exciting. On the whole, did your father bring you up to enjoy life, or not?

REITH No, there was great love from both my father and mother, but there was an austerity in my father's surroundings, and I never learnt that life was for living – do I make myself clear? I don't know that that has quite come to me even yet.

FREEMAN What is the most vivid picture you can see at this moment, thinking of those early days?

REITH My father preaching in the pulpit of the College church.

FREEMAN And what did he look like? A fine imposing man, was he like you in size?

REITH He was not quite as tall as I. He was six foot two and he was tremendously impressive.

FREEMAN And his voice?

REITH A most beautiful voice and a smile that was benign.

FREEMAN And he was in fact the most potent influence in your childhood days?

REITH Yes – no doubt at all.

FREEMAN Now, schooling. You've written about yourself that your schooling was, well, undistinguished. You went first to Glasgow Academy and then – rather curiously, I think – to Gresham's School in Norfolk. Did you find it easy in your schooldays to accept discipline from the masters, and also the disciplines of communal living among other boys?

REITH The latter more easily than the former. I was inclined to be a bit unruly.

FREEMAN Were you inclined to be resentful of schoolmasters, or not?

REITH Not in general, but of individuals.

FREEMAN Can you recall – looking back now on your schooldays – any particular landmark which was a turning-point in terms of success or of growing up?

REITH Going to an English boarding-school.

FREEMAN When you changed from Glasgow Academy?

REITH Yes. Glasgow Academy was, and is, a magnificent school, one of the very finest in the country, but it was the greater discipline and the communal living, that you refer to, of an English boarding-school that made a great deal of difference to me.

FREEMAN Lord Reith, tell me how tall you are?

REITH Six foot six when I stand straight.

FREEMAN Now, how old were you when you grew to that height?

REITH About twenty-three.

FREEMAN Did you at any stage outgrow your strength?

REITH Never . . . I've got too much strength, and have had all along, I think.

FREEMAN Do you look at other people and think, 'Well, I'm bigger than he is'?

REITH No, I usually wish I weren't as big as I am. It's awkward. Anything over six foot two is an affliction, Mr Freeman. Have you got that?

FREEMAN Yes, I have. Would you say of yourself – throughout your life – that you've been an ambitious man?

REITH Ambition, as normally understood, *absolutely* no. I'm incapable of the technique which ambition, in the ordinary sense, almost inevitably compels – the devices and expedients that it normally compels. I've been ambitious in this other sense – minded to do whatever came to one's hands with all one's might, both hands; better, to do whatever it was at least as well as anybody else could, and in shorter time. Is that clear? In other words to be fully stretched. Not ambitious for this or that position. Except in so far as this or that position would make one fully stretch, and all one's capacities and intelligence and strength used.

FREEMAN Can you remember how old you were when you first formulated that thought?

REITH About eighteen.

FREEMAN Was that when you first realised you had great powers of decision and ability to organise others, or were you younger when you first realised that?

REITH A little bit younger than that.

FREEMAN Can you remember the occasion vividly, or not?

REITH Yes. On the top of Ben Macdui in the Cairngorms in Invernessshire. I had just been climbing and climbing all day long, and wondering whatever I was going to do in the world. And the prospect was pretty bleak, because I didn't know what I wanted to do. I only felt conscious that I ought to be able to do all sorts of things, but how to set about them? Ignorant – and no help from anybody. I was about seventeen and a half.

FREEMAN And you did your apprenticeship as an engineer, and you went to the first war – did you get much of permanent value out of either of those experiences?

REITH Nobody can talk to me today about hours of work, or conditions of work, because I served a five-year apprenticeship in locomotive shops in Glasgow, and it was a very trying period. But it was of immense value in some ways. But whether there was more lost than gained, I wouldn't know.

FREEMAN In terms of wasting talent, do you mean?

REITH Yes – and time. Five years – getting up at a quarter to five every morning, except Sundays, and working from six o'clock till five-thirty, and most of the time three hours' evening classes, in the technical college every night.

FREEMAN Looking back, all these years later, at the work of constructing the BBC – because that's what you did – are you conscious of having made any substantial error of judgement or mistake in the edifice which you erected?

REITH No.

FREEMAN The distinguishing mark, really, was a publicly owned corporation which was not susceptible to government control. Did you have to battle to establish this independence from the government?

REITH At first, yes. The first decision to be taken was whether or not the British Broadcasting Company Limited should have its licence extended, after its first four years. It had a two-year licence, then a committee, which recommended another two years – that's four – and then I felt strongly that it should be turned into a public corporation – the first of its kind. And there was opposition to that. The BBC was in the hands of the wireless trade, but they had never dominated policy decisions or anything of that sort, they had left me virtually full freedom of management and allowed *me* to manage the BBC Company, in the interests of broadcasting and of the country. But there was a danger that the next Board of Directors might not be as broad-minded and far-seeing, and I felt that it should become a public corporation and I strongly urged that, with the permission of my own board, which was given – to their great credit, I think.

FREEMAN Yes, but once you'd got the charter, once that was established, did you then ever have to fight the government to make sure that your independence was maintained?

REITH Often. In the finance, that was the first of the things that we came on. As to the introduction of controversy. They gave me – us – a free hand as to staff. There was no attempt to interfere with salaries, we could pay any salaries we wanted. There was never any attempt to interfere with what was paid to artists, there was never any attempt to interfere with controversial happenings – like the introduction of the *Radio Times*, or, still more controversial, *The Listener*. They very nearly interfered, though – the Prime Minister personally – very nearly. That answer your question?

FREEMAN Yes. Did you – because in the end you did establish almost complete authority inside this corporation – did you consciously impose your own view of the world on the programmes and the practice of the BBC?

REITH That's a leading question, isn't it? Yes, but my own view was not just the product of my own imaginings, or principles, or characteristics. It was formed – there was a very large measure of devolution, and many senior executives were a party to the decisions which were taken.

FREEMAN Your own particular view, for instance, of religion, let's take that as an example, was the one that the BBC took collectively?

REITH It was taken by me and accepted by the others.

FREEMAN Yes. Now do you think it was good for any one man – however distinguished – however self-confident – to have so much control over what people were thinking and hearing?

REITH Do you remember, Mr Freeman, that I've said that there was a Board of Governors over me, in whom *de jure* all responsibility and authority was vested. I never claimed any *de jure* authority or responsibility – never. Although I might have an enormous amount, 99 per cent, given to me, not taken, given, *de facto*, by the board. They could intervene if they wanted to. They were given an opportunity of expressing themselves on all the major issues, and on several minor ones that were likely to attract attention. Do you see what I mean?

FREEMAN Yes, I do.

REITH Moreover, there was a very strong executive system. In my first six months I established what was called a Control Board, executives, meeting weekly, and it was unusual for decisions to be taken there merely because I said so. In other words, you might have asked me, 'Do you wish to have yes-men?' 'Of course I wish to have yes-men,' I might say, but yes-men who having expressed fully and freely and with any emphasis they liked their point of view, would accept mine even if it were different from theirs. Have I made that clear?

FREEMAN Yes, perfectly.

REITH Well, throughout, although undoubtedly I framed, formulated and saw to the execution of various policies, I would say, by and large, throughout, it was with the entire approval of the Board of Governors, which changed every now and again. And, by and large, with the approval of the senior executives.

FREEMAN Have you ever had any doubt in your mind, looking back since, that a form of public service monopoly is the right way towards organised broadcasting and television?

REITH Never. I think one of the most deplorable mistakes ever made in public affairs was made when the BBC monopoly was broken, I think it was shocking.

FREEMAN Yes, but a lot of the public would say that the BBC has improved greatly under the stimulus of competition from commercial television.

REITH All right, Mr Freeman. The public, by and large, were satisfied with the BBC as it was before the monopoly was broken. Anyhow, when I left it.

FREEMAN Are you sure the charges aren't true – which people have made, you know – that the BBC was a bit aloof, that it gave people what it thought they ought to have, rather than what they wanted? It wasn't too considerate of the wishes of the listeners and the viewers.

REITH If you're telling me that the BBC declined in competitive spirit, and energy, and imagination, after I left it, well I should be awfully sorry, but obviously I can't deny that.

FREEMAN There have, in fact, been a great many changes since you left. Do you regret them, or do you realise that they have perhaps been inevitable?

REITH A great many, I think, were not inevitable, and I regret them. I believe that a business of every sort, or almost every sort, depends on one man, whether he's executive chairman, or chairman, or general manager, or what – it depends on one man for its success. Well, if I'd answered that earlier it would be more relevant. I think that that's the point now. I hold that still.

FREEMAN How much do you yourself listen in and look at television?

REITH None at all.

FREEMAN Were you not interested in the programmes after you left?

REITH When I leave a thing, Mr Freeman, I leave it.

FREEMAN Well, I accept that, but I put it to you that if you do, it means that you were not passionately interested in the programmes in the first place.

REITH No, I don't think that's fair. I mean, inaccurate, not unfair. I was passionately interested in the programmes when I was in the BBC. My golly! I listened to them night after night. I got a weekly list of things from the head of the Programme Division that I had to listen to, I took that as an instruction. When I left the BBC maybe I didn't want to subject myself to unnecessary irritation, maybe I thought that I had better things to do.

FREEMAN When you left the BBC you were less than fifty and you were one of the most influential, responsible, and perhaps powerful men in Britain, and since then I should say you've had not very much influence, and no more responsibility than about a thousand other people could have exercised quite adequately. Now, do you agree with that?

REITH Absolutely.

FREEMAN How did it come about?

REITH A virtual collapse. Is that right?

FREEMAN Yes, quite right.

REITH I left the BBC and regretted it, profoundly. I thought it was fully well organised, capable of taking care of any development that came, war or anything. In other words, I wasn't busy enough. Is that understandable?

FREEMAN Yes, but have you ever been busy enough since?

REITH No, not qualitatively. Quantitatively, I think I'm more busy now than I've perhaps ever been in my life, but not qualitatively.

FREEMAN In wartime, what job would really have satisfied you?

REITH I regretted very much indeed, Mr Freeman, that Mr Churchill didn't give me ten times as much work and responsibility as he did. I believe I could have carried it, and I could have helped him enormously.

FREEMAN He, of course, wrote to you, you remember, later on and said that the story about you was that you were difficult to get on with; is that true?

REITH Yes, I suppose it is.

FREEMAN Other people are also difficult to get on with.

REITH Yes, other people. It may be to one's credit if one's difficult to get on with, isn't it? Should you tolerate inefficiency and slow-wittedness and all the rest of it?

FREEMAN Well, I think I should ask you that question. Do you tolerate slow-wittedness and inefficiency, easily?

REITH If you were asking me what mistakes I've made, that's one. That I haven't made enough effort to tolerate slow-wittedness, and all the rest of it.

FREEMAN What sort of person are you in your private life? I mean, are you patient with other people, on the whole, or not?

REITH I just don't know. I just don't know.

FREEMAN Would you say you've got a sense of humour?

REITH Yes, I have a sense of humour but not as much as I wish I had.

FREEMAN Do you bear grudges against people when they offend you?

REITH I can be unforgiving. There are some people whom I will not forgive, or anyhow haven't forgiven yet. I have a black list, and there are only about eight people on it, for all my long life.

FREEMAN I don't suppose you'd like to tell us who they are, would you?

REITH I'd better not. I've answered you awfully frankly so far, but I think I'd better keep that back. It isn't the same eight. I mean, somebody goes off, do you see, one year, somebody else goes off the next year, because I've managed to persuade myself, at long last, that there was a fault on my side. I try – that's at least honest, isn't it?

FREEMAN Very.

REITH – I try hard to persuade myself that it was more my fault than I could have realised. All right, then the man comes off, but somebody new, maybe, comes on.

FREEMAN Have you ever had a desire to take violent action?

REITH Only once. Unless I misunderstand you. My father at the age of seventy-three had been run over by a drunken van-driver one day, and I thought he wasn't going to recover. He was very badly hurt indeed. I went out to find the man, and I told the police inspector in the College Division that if I found the man I wouldn't be answerable for what happened. Now, I was extremely sure, in those days, but I took an inch-and-a-half spanner in my trouser pocket to make sure. That all right?

FREEMAN You really feel you would have used it?

REITH I hope I wouldn't have had to use an inch-and-a-half spanner, and even if I had I hope I wouldn't have killed a man, but I merely gave notice that I wouldn't be responsible for what happened. I'd have wrought vengeance on that man if I could have found him. Does that answer your question?

FREEMAN Yes, it answers it splendidly. Have you been happy, looking back on your seventy years?

REITH Oh no.

FREEMAN You've not been happy?

REITH No.

FREEMAN Have you been successful?

REITH No.

FREEMAN Well, in what does your lack of success consist, then? I mean, for instance, have you ever wanted political power?

REITH I have wanted to be fully stretched, Mr Freeman, and possibly the positions in which one would have been most fully stretched are political. Do you want me to be more specific?

FREEMAN Yes, I would like you to.

REITH I would like to have been Viceroy of India, I would like to have been Prime Minister, merely because, as far as I can see, there are one or two other jobs I might like now. But not for the power or patronage, or anything, but for the full stretching.

FREEMAN Reflecting on what, after all, you call failure, not I, what would you say your greatest defect of character has been?

REITH Not tolerating the individuals we were talking about earlier. Not going their pace instead of my own pace. Not taking an hour to do a job, instead of five minutes, because the hour was the average performance. Is that clear?

FREEMAN Yes, quite clear. You said just now that there were perhaps still a few jobs that you'd like to do. What are they?

REITH Oh, I couldn't name them. It would be awfully improper to, wouldn't it? Do you mind not?

FREEMAN But it's a public ambition of some kind that you feel you could still fulfil?

REITH Yes, absolutely. And one of the most difficult things of all. That is the attraction.

FREEMAN I'm going to put one last question to you now. Last year you were speaking at your old school, at Glasgow Academy, and you used these words, if I can quote them to you: 'I now realise', you said, 'how much I have missed, and how many mistakes I've made.' Well, just tell me what had you missed and what were the mistakes?

REITH That life's for living. That's what I've missed. And the mistakes I've alluded to – my keeping to my own pace, when I ought to have had the sense to slow down and take the average pace. Is that clear?

VICTOR GOLLANCZ

INTRODUCTION

The guest on *Face to Face* on 27 November 1960 was a man described by his friend John Strachey as 'publisher and author: capitalist and socialist: man of the world and latter-day saint: Jew and Christian: rationalist and theologian: rebel and traditionalist'. This jumble of contradictions was Victor Gollancz, founder, chairman and managing director of one of Britain's most successful and controversial publishing houses.

It was after the First World War that Gollancz first moved into publishing, later founding Victor Gollancz Ltd, in bare offices in Covent Garden, in 1928. Its first publication was Sherriff's indictment of the war, *Journey's End*, and among Gollancz's later discoveries were A. J. Cronin, Daphne du Maurier and Kingsley Amis. The ideological, rather than the business, element of publishing appealed to him most. He was well aware of the contradiction between the socialism he supported and the capitalism which provided the means for him to do so, and it was a paradox he acknowledged wryly in his *Face to Face* interview.

As well as being an active pacifist, feminist and socialist, Gollancz was a supporter of nuclear disarmament and founded the Association for World Peace, which we now know as War on Want. He was also foremost among those who, between the wars, helped prepare the ground for a Labour Party victory in 1945, and the subsequent introduction of a welfare state. (In 1936 he had launched the famous Left Book Club in an attempt to expose Nazism and avert the Second World War.)

Gollancz's religion, 'Judaeo-Christianity', was dwelt on at length in his *Face to Face* interview, and was seen to form the basis of many of his secular ideas. When discussing the abolition of capital punishment, the passion of the sixty-seven-year-old guest seems to have infected the traditionally faceless and unopinionated interviewer: Freeman was, for once in the series, moved to agree with him.

In 1965, Gollancz was knighted. He died in 1967 at the age of seventy-three, leaving his company in the hands of his eldest daughter. Gollancz may have suffered from a quick temper, egoism and material self-indulgence: that much is acknowledged by friends and critics alike. However, *The Times* obituary reflected the sentiments of many of those who had observed his life: that Victor Gollancz had been a phenomenon who 'would have made his mark in any age.'

INTERVIEW

FREEMAN Mr Gollancz, you are known to the world as a Jew, as a sort of Christian, as a sort of socialist, and as a rich, at any rate, a highly successful publisher. And I want to ask you, first of all, about being a Jew. Now, to what extent do you nowadays practise the observances of the Jewish religion?

GOLLANCZ I don't practise any of the more obvious observances. I do practise certain things in the old traditional Judaism which I think very beautiful – such as, for instance, giving thanks on eating the first fruit you particularly like in the year. When I enter a prison I say the old Jewish blessing, 'Blessed art Thou, O Lord, who looseneth the bound.' Things of that sort. I have also, up in my house, a thing called a *mezuza*, which is a little silver object with the first letter of the name of God appearing through the silver – the idea being that every house is a consecrated place. And I like to keep up these things which seem to me very good, reminding one that all life is holy. But the actual keeping the Sabbath, or anything of that kind, I have nothing to do with that whatever.

FREEMAN You never visit synagogues?

GOLLANCZ No, I haven't been in a synagogue since I married in 1919.

FREEMAN Now, would you say that being a Jew, in your feeling, is a matter of practice, the kind of things you do, or do you regard it as a matter of descent and of family tradition?

GOLLANCZ For me, I suppose, it means that while a great deal in traditional Judaism is not only unsympathetic but even perhaps rather obnoxious to me, there's a certain kind of way of looking at things – in particular, this idea that there is no real division between the holy and the unholy, the sacred and the profane, but that all life is in some sense sacred – I would say that that is a certain way of looking at things which I derive from a traditional Jewish background.

FREEMAN Yes. So that you would recognise for yourself some sort of private identity with other Jews which is denied, let's say, to me, and which is not merely a matter of attending synagogue together?

GOLLANCZ Yes, I would say that is so, yes.

FREEMAN I wonder how much you publicly identify – do you, for instance, rather self-consciously support Jewish charities?

GOLLANCZ Oh, no, no, I don't, no, no. I rather self-consciously don't support Jewish charities because there are so many rich Jews, who can do so, and in fact do so, but I like supporting the rather out-of-the-way things, the things nobody else supports.

FREEMAN When you're totally relaxed and off duty and sitting in your home, do you prefer the company of other Jews or are you not conscious at all of whether people are Jews or not?

GOLLANCZ Oh no. I'm not really conscious. I have no feelings of any kind about race or nationality. The more people are mixed, the better.

FREEMAN Yes. That isn't, of course, quite true, because you've just been admitting and describing a certain racial distinction that you yourself find in being a Jew.

GOLLANCZ Yes, but that is a sort of flavour, which I happen to have, but I equally appreciate, because I have that flavour, most other flavours, too.

FREEMAN Do you think that British Jews ought to try to assimilate completely – do you think they've done so, for instance?

GOLLANCZ They haven't done so. I do think so, yes. I believe in complete assimilation. Although, of course, people sometimes think that's a paradox, when I say that, because this particular flavour that I've spoken of would vanish. But I'd sooner that vanished than that separatism remained.

FREEMAN Well, are you conscious at all of being a member of a minority group in British society as it is constituted today?

GOLLANCZ No, it doesn't obtrude itself on me in any kind of way.

FREEMAN You probably have less of a chip on your shoulder than almost any other man living, but would you think it not unreasonable that very many Jews do feel very consciously a member of a minority and slightly oppressed group?

GOLLANCZ Yes, I think that's quite natural.

FREEMAN Did you feel that, for instance, in your childhood at school, let's say?

GOLLANCZ No, not at all, because I was at St Paul's, and there was a very large, specially large, percentage of Jews at St Paul's and all sorts of special arrangements were made for them. But I felt something quite different, I did feel that they were free in some ways which I wasn't free.

FREEMAN What, the Gentile boys were free?

GOLLANCZ Yes, the Gentile boys were free in a way in which I wasn't free.

FREEMAN But you never had this agony which some Jewish boys have of being half persecuted at school?

GOLLANCZ Oh dear me, no! I wasn't in the least persecuted.

FREEMAN Now, could we just talk about your childhood for a bit, because it's a very marked contrast with the liberal professions that you follow today, I think. You were brought up in a very orthodox home –

GOLLANCZ An orthodox but not an ultra-orthodox.

FREEMAN – in an orthodox, but not ultra-orthodox, home, from which you fairly early began to revolt?

GOLLANCZ Very early.

FREEMAN Well, when were you first conscious of it?

GOLLANCZ Oh, I don't know – I was very precocious – I suppose at about six, six or seven.

FREEMAN What was it that you found oppressive, particularly?

GOLLANCZ Well, I found all the business about not working on the Sabbath absolutely idiotic. I found the dietary laws, well, they were so compulsive that I still willy-nilly cling to a great number of them, even today, I found those stupid. I very early found the absolutely rigid fast on the Day of Atonement offensive. I suppose it was at quite an early age that I came to the conclusion that what was important on the Day of Atonement was not to fast, not to abstain from drinking, to the extent, in my father's case, of not even cleaning one's teeth, but what was important was to repent. This kind of thing, the sort of revolt I think St Paul had, the clash between the letter and the spirit which is really what –

FREEMAN Yes. St Paul, of course, was a bit older than six when he had it. . . . I'm just wondering if you can recall what set this off because it really is very precocious at the age of six.

GOLLANCZ I may be inventing this, I don't really know, but looking back I should have thought it might have been the lighting of fire on the Sabbath. I seem to remember that it was very cold one winter and there was a fire which hadn't been lit and I wanted to put a match to it, and my father said: 'You can't light fire on the Sabbath.' I'm rather inclined to think that that was the first occasion on which the sheer irrationality of the thing occurred to me, that you can't do a thing.

FREEMAN Do you have any memory of resentment or clashing with your father on some issue of that kind which is still traumatic today?

GOLLANCZ No, no particular one.

FREEMAN You talked about dietary laws . . .

GOLLANCZ No Gentile, I think, could possibly understand how compulsive taboos, like the food taboos, are. I do remember, for instance, saying to my father once: 'Do you think it more wicked to commit a murder than to eat pork?' And I remember my father answering: 'Of course, it's morally worse to commit a murder, but the difference is this – I could commit a murder, and I couldn't conceivably eat pork.' That, I think, explains the force of the taboo, and that, in fact, has persisted in me, because although I'm completely emancipated in all those ways, and although I can just manage, in fact, I can even rather enjoy very crisp bacon, all other forbidden food, such as pork, or loathsome things like oysters and shellfish, and so on, I just cannot possibly touch.

FREEMAN Tell me a little bit about your father – was he a very dominant character?

GOLLANCZ No. He was an obstinate man. Looking back on him I think he was a very lovable man, although I didn't greatly love him at the time. He was an immensely honourable man, worked frightfully hard for his family –

FREEMAN He was what, a small business man?

GOLLANCZ He called himself a wholesale jeweller . . . I think he was really what one might nowadays call a middleman, between the retailer and the wholesalers. He worked exceedingly hard. He was a man of considerable charm, but no, he was quite gentle but immensely intolerant, which is, of course, quite a different thing. I mean, the suggestion, for instance that we could break any of these Jewish taboos would be absolutely horrible to him.

FREEMAN One always thinks that the absolute basis of Jewish family life is deep respect for the father and mother. Well, you felt some respect, but could you define your attitude a little more closely – were you afraid of him at all?

GOLLANCZ Oh no, not in the least afraid, not in the least afraid. I had a sort of intellectual passion against him – I think that's the way to put it. I had a great intellectual passion, revolting against the anti-feminist treatment of my sisters, and I even remember having an intellectual passion against his reading of the *Daily Telegraph* and in revenge I took in the *News Chronicle*. It was this sort of almost impersonal thing – this man is wrong, he's absolutely wrong.

FREEMAN A good many Jews are probably made into radicals and rebels by the pressures of Gentile society outside, but it's quite clear that you were turned into a rebel by the pressures of your own orthodox family?

GOLLANCZ Entirely, yes – entirely.

FREEMAN I'd like to follow some of the main streams of rebellion now, that you've engaged in. I mean, Christianity, to begin with, which you've been interested in – since when?

GOLLANCZ Oh, I suppose since about the age of eleven or twelve when I first read the New Testament.

FREEMAN What was the particular –what shall I say – fish-hook which engaged your –

GOLLANCZ Oh, the Sermon on the Mount.

FREEMAN Was it the Sermon on the Mount that caught your imagination with talk about, for instance, poverty and mercy and so on, or was it an intellectual conviction that people ought to live in this way?

GOLLANCZ No, I should have thought the first, rather than the second – definitely the first. I definitely said, This is right – not what my father said, but this is right.

FREEMAN But there wouldn't have been a New Testament in Elgin Avenue?

GOLLANCZ Oh dear me, no! The New Testament for my father would definitely have been wicked, though by that curious paradox which you often find in Jews, I think if anybody had told him that Christ was a great man, and Christ, after all, was a Jew, he'd have been rather glad. I think his phrase would have been, 'Very nice.'

FREEMAN And you've always seen Christianity as being a kind of logical extension of Judaism?

GOLLANCZ Always, yes.

FREEMAN Are you particularly happy with the mystical nature of the Christian communion, and the Trinity, and so on, does that make a psychological appeal to you?

GOLLANCZ Curiously enough, the Trinity makes rather an intellectual appeal to me, I think it's quite a good philosophical scheme. But generally, you see, the genuinely mystical tradition is the same in all religions. The Jewish mysticism you find in the Cabala, in the *Zohar*, the tradition you find in the great Christian mystics, in the Muhammadan, it's all identical, and I am very, very sympathetic with it, because I do feel a good deal of it myself.

FREEMAN Have you found it possible, out of this strict Jewish background, to accept the notion of the divinity of Jesus Christ? Do you believe that?

GOLLANCZ I don't believe that I can give the sort of short answer that you would find satisfactory. But I once expressed it in this way, that there is the absolute and the particulars – the Platonic idea, the absolute good and the particular goods – well I think of Christ as a supreme particular, that is the way I expressed it.

FREEMAN Why have you never quite been able to accept conversion to the Christian faith?

GOLLANCZ I did nearly at one time. I think largely because, having escaped from one church I didn't want to get into another. I'm a great anti-institutionalist, I detest institutions.

FREEMAN But you consciously live by Christian ethics now?

GOLLANCZ Let's say that when I remember to, I try to.

FREEMAN Why do you prefer them to Jewish ethics?

GOLLANCZ Forgiving your enemies was a possibility in quite remote Old Testament times, but to love your enemies is something completely new, and I think it is the whole secret of life, it takes morality into a new dimension. And that is an idea in which Christianity has taken a lead from Judaism.

FREEMAN Well now, I want to ask you, precisely following on that, about the next stream of your rebellion, if you like, which is pacifism – well, the rejection of violence, at any rate. When did you first begin to think of war as being the great evil?

GOLLANCZ I think it was on my sixth birthday, but it may have been my seventh. My parents had a very comfortable house in Elgin Avenue with a drawing-room, and it had what were then called occasional tables, and my father, although he was a considerable reader of classics, he actually bought two modern books a year, one was the novel of the moment, which he never read, but he always bought, just as he always went to the Royal Academy, and the other was any other book which had created a great stir, and there was one book on this occasional table called *Sixty Years a Queen*. He was a very great patriot, my father, he thought a great deal of the Queen. A record for I suppose the Diamond Jubilee, and I opened it at two facing pages with pictures, I suppose reproductions of drawings – one of the Charge of the Light Brigade at Balaclava and the other the Charge of the Heavy Brigade, and one man was slashing the head off another man, and this produced in me a feeling of intense and appalling horror. I sensed myself having my head slashed off, and I thought, If this is war then war is a most appalling evil, we must get rid of it.

FREEMAN It's an astonishing story. Have you always identified with suffering?

GOLLANCZ Always, yes. Yes, always.

FREEMAN Is this the basis now for your feelings, for instance, about capital punishment?

GOLLANCZ Entirely the basis of it, yes, entirely the basis. I agree with all the logical reasons against capital punishment, too, of course, and I don't believe it's a deterrent and all this kind of thing, but it is simply that I enter into the feelings of the man who's condemned, I think of him waiting during these three weeks, I think of him on the last night, and I think that any human being, or any state, should inflict this agony on other human beings is unspeakably evil.

FREEMAN Did you always hate all kinds of violence against the person – I mean what about boxing, and even rugby football and so on, at school? Corporal punishment at school?

GOLLANCZ Corporal punishment I detested, I've always thought it a combination of beastliness and cruelty. Rugby football, I wouldn't feel anything wrong about that.

FREEMAN When you decided after the first war, and after a period of schoolmastering, to go into publishing, was the notion really that you'd have a greater opportunity to express your views?

GOLLANCZ Yes, entirely, entirely, yes.

FREEMAN And, of course, much of your publishing has, as everybody knows, been identified with political pamphleteering, but I notice that you've been a jolly prosperous commercial publisher as well. I mean, Daphne du Maurier, *Journey's End*, Kingsley Amis, Dorothy Sayers – you like business, don't you?

GOLLANCZ No, I hate it. I hate the business side – bargaining with authors, bargaining with agents, all that kind of business I detest. The reason why when I went into publishing I decided to cast my net wide and publish best-sellers if I possibly could was because I don't believe in running propaganda on a shoestring. If you want to do good through publishing, because you want to publish certain things, I believe in having the resources to do so, and I don't believe in being very austere about it and saying, I'll only publish this, I'll only publish that. Let's publish it all, provided it's not offensive in any kind of way, provided it reaches a certain standard, and we'll hope we'll make enough money on the swings to pay for the rather more important roundabouts.

FREEMAN Do you in fact briefly enjoy the luxurious things of life yourself?

GOLLANCZ Yes.

FREEMAN Food, drink, paintings . . .

GOLLANCZ Yes, yes, yes, yes.

FREEMAN What's your favourite relaxation?

GOLLANCZ Well, I don't know whether you'd call it a relaxation, of course, my favourite pursuit is listening to music, far and away . . . I wouldn't call it a relaxation, at all. I mean, it's far more serious than that, it's an act of communion.

FREEMAN In a perfectly innocent way you're self-indulgent in small ways – do you enjoy spending money on yourself, for instance?

GOLLANCZ No, I spend practically no money on myself – very, very little. I'm always thought to be self-indulgent because I frequently lunch at the Savoy, but as a matter of fact I actually spend on lunch at the Savoy very much less than most people, because as I entertain a lot there they let me have my plate of roast beef and my fried potatoes, and an inadequate tip, and don't bother me for a drink or anything, and I'm into the place and out of it within ten minutes. That's not really a sign of luxurious living, though I like good food immensely.

FREEMAN Well now, pursuing a little further your lines of rebellion, we come to socialism, and I want to ask you first of all, what do you mean by socialism?

GOLLANCZ Oh, by socialism I mean something quite different, I'm afraid, from any of the ordinary meanings of the word. I really mean living with a community of goods, the kind of socialism that used to be true, and perhaps still is true of the life in the kibbutzim in Israel. I don't quite believe in equal incomes because the people with beastly jobs ought to be paid more than the other people.

FREEMAN Well now, how honest is that? You don't pay the people with beastly jobs more in your business?

GOLLANCZ No, not at all, of course I don't. I don't think it's possible in the midst of a capitalist society to live according to the tenets of the kind of socialism which I hold. Obviously you can't have all things in common under the capitalist state, or in the kind of state that masquerades as a socialist state. I'm simply telling you what I really believe in . . . above all, I believe in an approach to that kind of spirit, the spirit of selflessness, the spirit of the absence of greed, and so on, and of course a great deal of modern socialism is simply inverted greed – it's better than capitalist greed because the people have been down and out and have had nothing, but morally it's the same . . . the most for yourself.

FREEMAN Are you yourself greatly moved by the sight of poverty, is that an identification?

GOLLANCZ Very greatly. When I was first going to St Paul's, when I was about thirteen, and I had to go by train to Hammersmith, and I used to see these appalling houses, with dustbins and decaying fish-heads and all this kind of thing in the yard, and I used to think how awful it must be for people to live like that while I'm going home to my comfortable tea, lying on a sofa and eating raspberry jam sandwiches and so on, and again it was a question of identification – loathing of this kind of poverty.

FREEMAN Looking back on all the causes that you've supported, the Left Book Club, collective security, helping the Germans after the war, helping the Jews during the war, the whole lot of your causes, which is the one which you feel has really been closest to your heart?

GOLLANCZ Oh, the abolition of capital punishment. Far and away. However decayed I become, I propose not to rest until we have finally abolished this frightful scandal from our midst.

FREEMAN Well, as it happens I agree with you, but this is a very small cause in a world which is absolutely full of disaster, isn't it?

GOLLANCZ Yes, but it's a thing, first of all, which we can do ourselves. I mean the great world situation, I can't personally do anything about that, except to try and spread tolerance and this kind of thing about, but I can do something in the matter of capital punishment. I believe that I, and those who think like me, between us can abolish the thing, and that is why it really means most to me.

FREEMAN Now, comes the time when I have to put a final question to you, and listening to you I was struck by the conflict between what some people have called the saintly side of your nature, at any rate the side of public ideals and so on, and the fact that you have obviously been a very successful business man. I don't know whether you would ever claim to be a saint, perhaps not, but if I were the devil's advocate, and the question of your canonisation was under discussion I would perhaps say that you'd done very well in a wicked world, and I would wonder whether you hadn't perhaps worked too closely with Mammon quite to have succeeded in furthering the God that you –

GOLLANCZ Oh undoubtedly! I am an exceeding weak human being with a great liking for the good things of this world and I would say a hundred times, I have compromised too much with Mammon, in fact, if I were summoned before the heavenly tribunal and I were taxed with that I think I'd prefer to be silent.

ADAM FAITH

INTERVIEW

On 11 December 1960, some of the viewers who switched on their televisions to watch *Face to Face* did so with a feeling of anticipated distaste. The programme was by now famous for its interviews with distinguished personalities, philosophers and men and women of letters – the likes of Lord Birkett, Dr Jung, Dame Edith Sitwell and Evelyn Waugh. This time the guest was a twenty-year-old 'pop' star, who had recently topped the charts with his first solo hit 'What Do You Want If You Don't Want Money?'.

The programme showed Faith to be articulate, thoughtful and charming, and he relished the experience. Afterwards he described it as 'a pleasant talk with a very pleasant man', and later claimed that the programme had a remarkable impact on his whole career: 'Suddenly, in a sense, I became establishment, acceptable to the establishment.' The newspapers reported that, 'Adam seems to have done himself more good by *talking* than by *singing*', and that he had emerged as 'a wise and wily 20-year-old'. The reaction of most viewers, canvassed after the programme, was one of agreeable surprise. One retired business man confessed: 'It taught me a lesson not to prejudge a generation with which I am not in personal contact.'

Adam Faith's pop-singing career, at its zenith at the time of *Face to Face*, was to be short-lived and in 1968 he abandoned the pop business. In the meantime, at the age of twenty-seven – a little younger than he had suggested in his *Face to Face* interview – he had married his wife Jackie. Faith then – as he had predicted – trained as an actor and joined a repertory theatre, where Dame Sybil Thorndike praised his talent, and *Budgie*, the popular 1970s television series, brought him national fame once again.

The twenty-year-old Faith, anxious to take the best professional advice about how to manage his money, already showed signs of the astute business man he was later to become. Nowadays he is a director of The Savoy, he has his own financial advisory service and he writes a weekly business column in a national newspaper.

Seeing, for the first time, his twenty-year-old self talking on *Face to Face*, Faith commented recently that it was as though he was watching another person. In fact, many would argue that the young Adam, with his love of a challenge, sound financial awareness, down-to-earth attitudes and enduring amiability, was already sowing the seeds of long-term stardom.

INTERVIEW

FREEMAN Adam Faith, at the age of twenty, you are for my money the number one pop singer in this country today. At least two of your records have sold more than half a million copies, you earn about ten times as much as a cabinet minister, I understand. Every time you show yourself in public you risk being physically injured by your fans. Now that's an odd life for a young man of twenty. Tell me, taking it by and large do you enjoy being a star?

FAITH Mainly, I love it.

FREEMAN What do you like best about it?

FAITH First and foremost I like the independence of the life, I like the glamour, I like the feel of the audience – I like the luxury.

FREEMAN You think you have achieved independence, do you?

FAITH Well, personal, mental independence I have, yes. Physical independence, of course, no.

FREEMAN No. Well now, let's look at your life as a star for a bit. How many secretaries and managers and agents and musical advisers and all the rest of it do you have?

FAITH Well, I have four people working on the fan club, one full-time and the other three part-time. I have a manager and an agent, I have a musical adviser. That's about it.

FREEMAN You're very dependent on your manager?

FAITH I trust her completely. If I didn't, well, we wouldn't be able to work.

FREEMAN Do you take advice on your life apart from your professional work?

FAITH I listen to advice, whether I take it is another matter.

FREEMAN But at any rate, it's offered and you listen to it with respect?

FAITH Oh yes.

FREEMAN Do you choose your own songs that you record or does she choose them for you?

150

FAITH No, I choose all the material.

FREEMAN So the successes and the failures – there aren't any so far, but still – that's all your responsibility?

FAITH Yes.

FREEMAN How hard do you work now? I mean, when did you last have a week off?

FAITH Well, it wasn't so long ago actually. I went to Spain for six days – maybe ten weeks ago.

FREEMAN And is that the only holiday you've had this year?

FAITH Apart from a few odd days, yes.

FREEMAN Now, this does seem a very heavy work cycle, because I think you've only made seven discs including your long-player, haven't you?

FAITH Yes – well, six successful records, an LP and three unsuccessful ones.

FREEMAN I didn't know about the unsuccessful ones.

FAITH I keep them very quiet.

FREEMAN What takes up all this time, it can't be making seven records?

FAITH Oh no. It takes maybe a few hours in a recording studio to cut a disc. But when we're on one-night stands I get to the theatre at seven-thirty and leave at ten-thirty, then go to the hotel, sleep, get up the next morning and travel the whole day to the next venue.

FREEMAN Do you find that you're recognised wherever you go in hotels?

FAITH Fortunately, yes.

FREEMAN Fortunately?

FAITH Well, when people stop recognising me, I shall start to worry.

FREEMAN Yes. Now tell me a bit about this fan club.

FAITH Well, every month they send out a newsletter, and the girl, Angela, she gets the fans together, she organises coach trips, if they ask for photographs she gives them photographs, and all sorts of things.

FREEMAN How many letters do you get each week?

FAITH Well, I don't know, I never ask Angela that.

FREEMAN Do you never answer the letters?

FAITH A few – when I get them at the theatre, I answer some myself. But it would be impossible to answer all of them.

FREEMAN How many times do you have to sign your autograph in a week, do you know?

FAITH Well I counted one week, and I kept it up for three days and it was over 700, so I gave it up then.

FREEMAN Yes, I see. You said just now that you liked being recognised, but nevertheless this must limit your life very much? Can you take a girl out for an evening, for instance?

FAITH If I take her to dinner somewhere in a quiet restaurant, that's OK, if we go for a drive in the car, that's OK. But apart from that we don't go too far.

FREEMAN Do you make friends among your fans?

FAITH A few of them, but the trouble with that is I'm never at one place long enough to get familiar with them, so it's very difficult.

FREEMAN Would you like to marry?

FAITH Eventually, yes.

FREEMAN But not yet?

FAITH No.

FREEMAN Is that because your manager won't let you?

FAITH Well, I don't have any of those sort of clauses in my contract, you see.

FREEMAN It is, however, supposed to be very bad for a pop singer to be married, isn't it?

FAITH So I'm told, yes.

FREEMAN But you don't want to in any case yet awhile?

FAITH Well, I don't feel prepared for marriage just yet. Maybe thirty seems to be a good age. I don't know – you can't tell about those things, can you?

FREEMAN You wait – you'll find out.

FAITH It happens all of a sudden and that's it.

FREEMAN Let me ask you a bit about the finances of this big business and all the people it employs. It's said quite often that you earn about £1000 a week and, as you don't deny that, I suppose that's perhaps about true.

FAITH Yes, it is true to a certain extent. It's difficult to average out what one earns in a week, because of records, you get a royalty on them, and you get that in a lump sum, for a film you get that in a lump sum, so it's very difficult.

FREEMAN Quite. But still, if we divided a year's earnings by fifty-two, I daresay it would come to something like £1000 a week.

FAITH I should think so – yes.

FREEMAN Good. Well now, do you have professional advice as to what you do with that?

FAITH Well, I have. I've been in the business now for just over a year, and I've taken advice from my manager and her business associates, and I've been saving for the past year, and intend to do so for another six or eight months.

FREEMAN When you say saving – I don't want to be impertinent about this – does that mean you're not investing it, you're just literally saving it in the bank, or does it mean you're putting it out into investments?

FAITH Next summer, that'll be the time when I start to invest. Then I shall buy the best brains possible –

FREEMAN To advise you how to do it – yes. Now, what do you think you're saving for?

FAITH Security of old age for my family I'd say.

FREEMAN Yes. What about this luxury that you enjoy, just from day to day, what form does it take?

FAITH Well, the greatest luxury for me is having a car – that's been fantastic for me.

FREEMAN An expensive car?

FAITH Fairly expensive, yes.

FREEMAN Do you like driving fast?

FAITH When it's safe to do so, yes.

FREEMAN You like to drive yourself if you can?

FAITH Drive myself all the time.

FREEMAN What other personal relaxations do you enjoy? I mean, for instance, do you enjoy music when you're not working?

FAITH Oh yes, all the time.

FREEMAN The newspaper cuttings say that you like classical music, now is that just a story or is it true?

FAITH Well, you see, I always take interviews myself and I never give out any press releases, so most of it – what you read in the newspapers – is true, if not just slightly exaggerated. But I do enjoy classical music.

FREEMAN What particular composer?

FAITH Sibelius and Dvořák I enjoy very much, Tchaikovsky I like.

FREEMAN Is this a fairly new interest, or have you liked that all your life?

FAITH No, well, I've liked it for the past five years. My brother introduced me to classical music – he's ten years older than myself and he's always had a love for classical music, and I just picked it up from him.

FREEMAN Do you ever have time to go to a classical concert?

FAITH I haven't been to a classical concert for about nine months, the last one I went to see at the Royal Festival Hall – Toscanini.

FREEMAN Have you ever had any musical lessons?

FAITH Never.

FREEMAN Can you read music?

FAITH No.

FREEMAN What about jazz, do you like that or not?

FAITH Don't like too much jazz at all, just very selective pieces of modern and traditional jazz I like.

FREEMAN Any particular jazz man that you favour?

FAITH Traditionally I like Chris Barber very much, in fact I've always been a fan of Chris Barber, and modern jazz – well, it's very difficult to say because I've never collected modern jazz, I've just liked certain pieces, like the theme music from Peter Gunn's show, and Johnny Staccato – that type of thing.

FREEMAN Do you spend a lot on clothes?

FAITH Not too much, just what I need.

FREEMAN Do you worry about what you look like, to be properly dressed for the right occasion?

FAITH Oh yes, I always try to dress for the occasion.

FREEMAN Have you ever been present on some occasion when you've really felt out of place because you were in the wrong clothes?

FAITH Well, I have, actually.

FREEMAN Tell me – go on –

FAITH I went to the Dorchester for the Variety Club Luncheon, and I had to go to rehearsal in the morning because I was singing a song there, and I went in casual jacket and casual shirt, and I thought I had plenty of time to go home and put a tie on, and before I knew it the luncheon had started. And I was the only one there without a tie – out of I don't know how many hundreds of people. So that was a bit embarrassing.

FREEMAN It was probably very popular, in fact.

FAITH Yes, well, I don't know. They were all a lot older than me.

FREEMAN Do you read a lot?

FAITH Fair amount, yes. As much as I can.

FREEMAN Again, any particular tastes?

FAITH Well, I'm very varied again, I've read some of Huxley's books.

FREEMAN Aldous Huxley? Yes.

FAITH And – have you ever read any of Salinger's?

FREEMAN Yes, *The Catcher in the Rye.*

FAITH Yes – that's my favourite book. I'm going to start on Hemingway and Steinbeck now.

FREEMAN Do you read ever because you think you ought to read something, or do you always read just because you enjoy it?

FAITH Well, I started to read because I enjoyed it, but then I found so much benefit in reading and got so much from it that I determined myself to read as much as possible. And as varied as possible. Whenever I meet an interesting person I always try to pick their brains and find out what good books they've read, and what good music they've listened to lately, and I do it that way.

FREEMAN Now again, most of what we know about you is from reading the papers. It's said that you've suffered from bad health from time to time, that you've suffered from your nerves, that you've consulted psychiatrists, that you feel particularly nervous before shows and all the rest of it – how much of this is true?

FAITH Most of it is true, only exaggerated.

FREEMAN What about the psychiatrist, is that exaggerated?

FAITH Well, in fact, once I went.

FREEMAN Why?

FAITH Because I thought I was dying, I felt so mentally sick and tired – so I went along. And he said that I was overworking. But this was over two years ago.

FREEMAN Before you really hit the jackpot – before you were working anything like as hard as you are now?

FAITH Yes, a long while ago.

FREEMAN Now since you've had this great success, has all this problem become better or has it tended to be even more difficult?

FAITH Well, I've found that success has bred confidence for me, so don't suffer so much now.

FREEMAN So that even though you probably work very much harder you can still do it and get away with it all right?

FAITH Yes. I feel much easier now. I get nerves before I go on the stage every time.

FREEMAN Do you really like the world of show-biz, or do you still look back to a different world before you got this great success?

FAITH Well, I live a very personal life, away from show business.

FREEMAN When you're not on tour now where do you live?

FAITH I live at home with my parents.

FREEMAN Well, there's another young man in your life, of course, who isn't Adam Faith at all. Terry Nelhams. Now tell me a bit about Terry Nelhams, because I suspect he's a bit different perhaps from Adam Faith. How much are you with your family nowadays?

FAITH Very little now. I shall see them for the next ten weeks, because I'm working in Wimbledon in pantomime, and that's very near for me. I shall live at home.

FREEMAN When did you last see your parents?

FAITH A week ago, I came home for one night on a tour to go to a spastics ball. And I saw them that night.

FREEMAN Do you have a lot of local friends still round your own home, that haven't changed since you've become famous?

FAITH Before I went into show business I had four friends and I've still got them fortunately, and they've never changed at all towards me.

FREEMAN Now, you go home tonight, and tomorrow morning you'll wake up and you'll go outside and the local people in your own street will see you; will you be mobbed by fans then or do they accept you in your own home?

FAITH They accept me very much – I live on an estate of council flats, and having lived there for so long I haven't found any difference among them at all.

FREEMAN You're still Terry Nelhams to them?

FAITH Completely, yes.

FREEMAN Yes. Do you find any difference, any friction, between your present life and your family when you go home – I mean, for instance, do you keep different hours from what they do, do your parents go to bed early and you stay up half the night playing music, and that kind of thing?

FAITH Well, it's a little difficult in a small flat to play music because it keeps them awake –

FREEMAN That's just exactly what I'm asking you –

FAITH Yes, but I seldom sit up at home, because when I'm in Acton I spend time with my friends, and I go to their place to play music. So it doesn't interfere with my family. But I never went to bed before three or four o'clock before I came into the show business, so it hasn't made that much difference to them.

FREEMAN Do you ever ask your parents for advice now?

FAITH Well, they've never enforced their ideas on me, even at a young age, and now I suppose as I grow older, I didn't find I had to rely on them to live – you know what I mean? I started work when I was very young, I worked for my mother and I worked newspaper rounds when I was twelve, and I bought all my own clothes, so that I became independent very early on. And my mother and father encouraged it.

FREEMAN Yes. Do they take an interest in your career? They follow you and know exactly where you are and what you're doing?

FAITH Well, they'll be sitting home tonight watching this with a dry mouth –

FREEMAN Is your father a trade unionist?

FAITH No, he works for a coach company and I don't believe they have a union there.

FREEMAN Have you ever been a member of a union yourself?

FAITH Well, I'm a member of the ACTT, that's –

FREEMAN The Cine Technicians – and you've kept your card alive?

FAITH Yes.

FREEMAN Do you think you'll ever go back to it?

FAITH Well, you never know when you'll need it, you see. I don't know.

FREEMAN Tell me, when did you first discover – presumably as quite a kid – that you'd got this talent? Or were you grown up?

FAITH I was sixteen.

FREEMAN How did you discover it?

FAITH Well, I started as a messenger boy for a film company for a little while, there were six messenger boys, then I left the company and went to another, a television company to be an assistant editor –

FREEMAN A film editor?

FAITH Yes, a film editor. And the rest of the boys started a skiffle group, and they didn't have a singer, and so they asked me if I would come in the skiffle group and sing. And that was the first time. So I went down there and we rehearsed and practised and gradually it came about.

FREEMAN And your first professional engagement – was that *Six Five Special*?

FAITH Well, the very, very first professional engagement was at a boys' club in Wandsworth, I think we got fifteen shillings, and that was with the skiffle group.

FREEMAN *Six Five Special* was the first time you got two guineas anyway?

FAITH Yes, something like that.

FREEMAN You had two goes at this, didn't you?

FAITH Yes, I spent a couple of months in show business when I went on *Six Five Special*, I made two records and I did some stage shows and they were all deadly failures, so I got disheartened and went back to work. And then about a year later a good friend of mine, John Barry, rang me up at the film studios and said he was on a new BBC programme called *Drumbeat*, and they were looking for new faces on the show. So he fixed an audition for me with the producer, Stuart Morris, and I went along and Stuart gave me the show.

FREEMAN And that was your break?

FAITH That was when it first started.

FREEMAN Do you remember when you got that second offer? I mean, were you very excited about it, did you think, This time I'm going to be a star, or did you ask what's the money going to be, or what was in your mind?

FAITH Mostly . . . mostly I wanted a car, you see. And when I was in the film studios, I decided to devote myself to making a career and I became passionately interested in it, and I worked all hours, Saturday and Sunday, and before I knew it I had a small savings account – I think it was about thirty or forty pounds – and that decided me to save the rest to put a deposit on a car. So when I got this chance to go on *Drumbeat*, I kept my job for three weeks, and because the contracts were optional – three weeks, three weeks, nine weeks and then another thirteen, whatever it was, I decided to go on; if it wasn't a success, I'd made money off the three shows, I could buy a car – put a deposit down. But after three I got signed up for some more, so I gave up the job.

FREEMAN Yes. In other words the first impact was bankroll – it was a bit of a motor-car and so on?

FAITH Yes.

FREEMAN Is it still that? I mean, have you got a mission now, or are you still in this for the dough?

FAITH Well now – at first I was in it very much for the money, but that soon left me, because there's so much excitement and thrill connected with show business that after a while the money doesn't seem so important.

FREEMAN No, especially when you've got an awful lot of it. Do you worry about the future a lot?

FAITH I don't worry too much about the future, I have a little bit of money now.

FREEMAN Are you satisfied with the success you've had, or have you got a lot of ambitions that the world doesn't know about?

FAITH Well, I want to try and make better records, really I just want to become a better performer.

FREEMAN Yes, but how long do you reckon you can go on being a pop singer? Well, Bing's gone on a long time, of course, but do you really think you're going to spend your life singing, or are you going to develop into an actor, or do something quite different?

FAITH Well, I hope to sing for the rest of my life. But I want to spend much more time trying to develop as an actor.

FREEMAN Any notions of having any particular musical training or do you reckon you'll just allow yourself to develop as it comes?

FAITH Well, I think for a few years I'll just allow it to come. Because I don't know what makes people buy my records, it may be just the naturalness of the voice coming over, and if I take musical instruction it might destroy that, and I'd hate that to happen at this stage.

FREEMAN Do you get actual satisfaction yourself out of singing a song well?

FAITH Oh yes, as well as I can.

FREEMAN Yes. Now the image of you which is put across – you're quite different from most of the other pop singers. I've been consulting some teen-age friends of mine, and they tell me that you're cool, that you're moody, that you're mean, that you're off-beat, and you're sexually attractive. Well, is this the sort of image that you and your advisers want to create? It is different from the other pop singers, I think.

FAITH Yes. Well, it's very difficult to say here, because I don't have a press agent at all. And when I first started in show business I met Evelyn Taylor – my manager – and I dressed as I wanted to dress then, casually in jeans and a leather jacket, so I think that's the impression she got of me. And the press took it up because when I'm at rehearsal, that's how I dress. And I've always found that when I'm being interviewed, that they take the most outstanding characteristic, whether it's good or bad, or whether it's true or false, they just take that –

FREEMAN And blow it up –

FAITH – and that is the character that they build up. Then other pressmen read the cuttings that the first pressmen have built up, and they may go along to the interview and they've already got it sized up. You're fighting two battles.

FREEMAN What would you say is the most valuable lesson you've learned in your personal life in this – what is it – a year you've had of terrific success?

FAITH Well, I've become more tolerant to advice over this past year, because I came into show business knowing completely nothing and I only know just a little bit more now, and you need people to tell you where you're going wrong. I think I've relied on people to help me and it's overflowed into my personal life.

FREEMAN Now, looking at you from outside probably millions of teenagers would copy you whatever you did, if you shaved all your hair off like Yul Brynner a million young men would do this tomorrow morning. Now, do you think that makes sense, that a young man of twenty should be the idol of so many millions?

FAITH Sense – I don't know. You see, I don't feel that they would shave their heads if I had a Yul Brynner haircut. If I put my head in the gas oven, they wouldn't do it.

FREEMAN You think they're more independent than we give them credit for?

FAITH I meet teenagers all the time, and I've found them completely independent. In a world with many, many millions of people, and millions of teenagers, a few teenagers do things that get into the press, and immediately every single teenager in the country is put into the category.

FREEMAN Well now, let me ask you a last question. Whether they copy you or not, you're very much admired by millions of teenagers. Now, if you could say it for yourself, what are the qualities that you would most like to be admired for?

FAITH I think being an individual, being sincere and being frank with other people are the most important things.

MARTIN LUTHER KING

INTRODUCTION

The American civil rights leader Dr Martin Luther King was only thirty-two when he appeared in this *Face to Face* interview. Yet he was already the symbol of equality, justice and freedom for blacks. His peaceful sit-ins and protest marches had won a huge following across America. With his skilful rhetoric and inspiring personality, he was leading a new age of struggle against the appalling discrimination suffered by blacks in the American South.

For *Face to Face*, he flew over to London in 1961 especially to appear and he answered John Freeman's questions with dignity and eloquence, telling a compelling story of his private sacrifices and public humiliations – the countless arrests, the bombings and the assaults which were part of his daily life.

Two years after the interview, Martin Luther King gave his famous 'I Have A Dream' speech, delivered to the largest civil rights demonstration the United States had ever seen. The address combined his talents as a Southern Baptist preacher, with his faith as a Christian, to stir his supporters throughout the world. In 1964, he won the Nobel Peace Prize, the youngest person ever to receive the award.

But four years later, he was shot dead in Memphis, Tennessee. His last address there – just before his assassination at the age of thirty-eight – had been prophetic. 'I've been to the mountain-top,' he said. 'I may not get to the promised land with you, but I want you to know tonight, that we as a people will.'

Martin Luther King's memory is widely celebrated in America today – there is even a national holiday in his name, and numerous institutions, libraries and foundations committed to his work. This *Face to Face* interview is an important part of the archive that reveals the man himself.

INTERVIEW

FREEMAN Dr King, the most unexpected thing about you, to me, is that for a long time you've been a national leader of your people – you're one of the most influential figures, I suppose, in the United States – and yet you're only thirty-two years old. Now, did you have any special training for this kind of leadership when you were a boy?

KING No, I really didn't. I went through the discipline of early elementary school education and then high school and college and theological training, but never did I realise that I would be in a situation where I would be a leader, in what is now known as the civil rights struggle of the United States.

FREEMAN Is your father, who's also a Baptist pastor, as I know, is he a social reformer as well as a minister, or is he less interested in this side of it?

KING He is a pastor of a large church in Atlanta, Georgia, and he has had a strong interest in civil rights. He has been president of the National Association for the Advancement of Colored People in Atlanta, and he always stood out in social reform.

FREEMAN Do you think he saw that you would be a leader? Do you think he did, in fact, bring you up in some special way to face these responsibilities?

KING Well, after I decided to enter the ministry, he constantly stressed the need for leadership, and I'm sure that he hoped that I would stand out in this area. Whether he realised that I would do it or not is something else, but he certainly hoped for this.

FREEMAN What sort of home did you have as a child? Was it a strict home, for instance?

KING Well, I guess it was relatively strict. I faced the discipline that you would face in the very fervent religious background. However, I don't think it was over-strict to the point that I developed any personality conflicts as a result of my early childhood, but it was strict enough for me to develop certain disciplinary principles as I came up.

FREEMAN Were you a quick starter at your lessons?

KING Yes, I would say generally I was. Interestingly enough I didn't start out with an interest to enter the ministry – after I finished at high school I was interested in going into law, and also medicine, at one point, and all along I received fairly good grades, but finally I decided to enter the ministry and then went on to theological school.

FREEMAN Well now, when you were still a small boy, before those decisions came along, were you conscious of colour discrimination in your own life?

KING Yes, I became conscious of colour discrimination at a relatively early age. I think the first time was when I was about six years old. I had some friends, two white boys, and they were my inseparable playmates for the early years of my life, and I remember when I was about six something started happening, when I went over to play with them they always made excuses, they could not play, they were busy, and finally I went to my mother with this problem, and she tried to explain to me in the best way she could explain to a child six years old. And this was really the first time that I became aware of the racial differences – of the racial problem. She made it clear to me that this system had a long history, dating back to the time of slavery. She tried to explain the meaning of the system of segregation, but the thing I will always remember is that in the midst of her explanation she said to me, 'You must never feel that you are less than anybody else. You must always feel that you are somebody, and you must feel that you are as good as anybody else.' And of course this came up with me, in spite of the fact that I still confronted the system of segregation every day.

FREEMAN Was that a violent conflict in your life? If you really believed your mother and yet the system round you suggested that this wasn't true, it must have set up some sort of strain?

KING Yes, I think so. As I look back over those early days, I did have something of an inner tension. On the one hand my mother taught me that I should feel a sense of somebodiness . . . on the other hand, I had to go out and face the system, which stared me in the face every day saying, 'You are less than –' 'You are not equal to –' So this was a real tension within.

FREEMAN What were you really prevented from doing that a white child might have done?

KING Well, in my days in Atlanta as a child there was a pretty strict system of segregation. For instance, I could not use the swimming-pools . . . until the YMCA was built, a Negro YMCA, and they had a swimming-pool there, but certainly a Negro child in Atlanta could not go to any public park. I could not go to the so-called white schools, there were separate schools. And I attended a high school in Atlanta, which was the only high school for Negroes in the city. And this was a real problem because in Atlanta there are more than 200 000 Negroes. In many of the stores downtown, to take another example, I could not go to a lunch counter, to buy a hamburger or a cup of coffee, or something like that. I could not attend any of the theatres – only one or two Negro theatres. . . . They were very small. By and large, there was a very strict system of segregation and there was nothing called racial integration at that time in Atlanta.

FREEMAN Now, that's a description of the system. Was anybody actually cruel to you or violent to you because you were coloured?

KING Yes, we did confront some of those problems. I remember as a child seeing problems of police brutality and this was mainly aimed at Negro children and Negro adults. I can remember also the organisation that was known as the Ku Klux Klan – this is an organisation that stands on white supremacy and an organisation that, in those days, even used violent methods to preserve segregation and to keep the Negro in his place, so to speak. Now I can remember seeing the Klan actually beat Negroes on some of the streets there, in Atlanta.

FREEMAN But nobody ever beat you personally?

KING No. I did have one experience which was relatively minor but it still lived with me a great deal. When I was about eight years old I was in one of the downtown stores of Atlanta and all of a sudden someone slapped me, and the only thing I heard was somebody saying: 'You're that nigger that stepped on my foot.' And it turned out to be a white lady, and of course I didn't retaliate at any point. I finally went and told my mother what had happened and she was very upset about it, but at that time the lady who slapped me had gone, and my mother and I left the store almost immediately.

FREEMAN Can you remember at this distance of time why you didn't respond in any violent way?

KING Well, I think probably it was a combination of two things. I hadn't thought of non-violence at that early age, as a system of thought, or as a practical technique. I think a great part of it was that I wouldn't dare retaliate or hit back when a white person was involved, and I think some of it was a part of my native structure, so to speak; that is, I have never been one to hit back too much.

FREEMAN Well now, that's all, what, twenty years or so ago, I suppose . . . but how bad is the complaint today? The United States has changed a lot, the Negroes' rights are protected under the law, how much has this system changed between then and now?

KING Well, it has changed a good deal. It is far from what it ought to be but I can see many, many changes that have taken place over the last few years. For instance, in the same Atlanta, Georgia, which is one of the largest cities in the south, there are some Negro students in formerly all-white schools. Some of the parks are integrated. Just a few weeks ago, about 177 lunch counters were open to Negroes on a thoroughly integrated basis. I think I could say also that court injustice is not as glaring a reality today as it was ten years ago. Police brutality has diminished a great deal. So that in Atlanta alone there are many changes and when I look over the total situation I can say the same thing. For instance, when the United States Supreme Court rendered the decision declaring segregated schools unconstitutional in 1954 seventeen states and the District of Columbia practised segregation in the public schools, but today most of these states have made some move toward integration. Only three states are holding out, Mississippi, Alabama and South Carolina. So that there has been a great change since, say, 1950 or 1945.

FREEMAN Now it follows from that that you're not content that the Negro gets justice in the United States as things are at present, and you're not certain that the police do not victimise him?

KING Well yes . . . I think we have moved on a great deal but we still face token integration. By token integration I mean, a few Negroes getting justice in a particular situation, but the vast majority still confronting problems of economic insecurity, and social isolation. So that the problem now is to move from token integration to overall integration where it involves more than just a few students in a school, more than just a few lunch counters opened, more than gaining justice in the courts in a few situations, but in every situation.

FREEMAN You spoke a moment ago about having been thrust forward into this position of leadership. How exactly did it happen? Why are you at thirty-two virtually the leader of the Negroes in the United States?

KING I started out as a pastor in Montgomery, Alabama. After I finished my graduate work in Boston I returned to Montgomery to pastor a church. After I had been in Montgomery about a year, we had the problem there of facing many indignities and injustices on the city buses. Negroes were treated in a very discourteous manner, the bus drivers usually talked to Negro passengers in a very inhuman way, and not only that, the first ten seats were reserved for whites only, and even if Negro passengers packed the buses and the other seats, and there were no more seats left, other than these seats reserved for whites only, Negro passengers could not sit there. So they had to stand over these seats, even if a white passenger was not on the bus. Not only that, there were times when Negro passengers got on the buses at the front and put the fare in the box and then they had to get off the bus and board by the rear entrance. These were some of the conditions that existed and on the 5th December in 1955, a Negro woman was arrested, a Mrs Rosa Parkes, for refusing to give up her seat for a boarding white male passenger. Pretty soon after she was arrested the word got around the Montgomery community and there was a spontaneous reaction. I think I could say safely that more than 99 per cent of the Negro people of Montgomery rose up with a bit of indignation, righteous indignation, I would say, and this led to the bus boycott. The Negro citizens decided not to ride the buses until these conditions were changed. They asked me to serve as the spokesman and the president of the Montgomery Improvement Association, and from this time I found myself in a leadership position in the civil rights struggle.

FREEMAN And the bus boycott was, of course, a startling success, under your leadership?

KING Yes, we struggled for 381 days, but at the end of that we returned to thoroughly integrated buses, and they are integrated today in Montgomery.

FREEMAN Now, what has this position of leadership cost you in personal terms? I mean, are you threatened? Do you get anonymous letters? You have had violence, I think, shown to you, more than once. Tell us a little of what is involved in all that.

KING There was a time when we received as many as thirty and forty threatening calls a day, and, of course, I received numerous threatening letters. They say such things as: 'You are causing too much trouble in this town and if you aren't out within ten days you and your family will be killed.' Now, in Montgomery our home was bombed twice, and I guess these were the most severe instances of violence that we confronted, but even today we still confront threats in telephone calls and through the mail.

FREEMAN Have you found that the police have been diligent in protecting you, as diligent as they would be with a white leader?

KING Well, in Montgomery, Alabama they were not. Certainly we got no protection from the law enforcement agencies. In fact, one of the big problems that we confront in some situations in the south is that many of the mobs and the hoodlums are aided and abetted by some of the policemen. But I must say that this is a little different in Atlanta, Georgia. When we have received threats, when we have had crosses burned on our lawn by the Ku Klux Klan, the policemen have been very diligent in attempting to protect us. So that situations do vary even in the Deep South.

FREEMAN You were once the victim of an actual assassination attempt, were you not? What happened?

KING Well, this was in Harlem, it turned out to be a demented Negro woman. She happens to be in an institution, even at this hour, for the criminally insane. I was autographing books in a bookstore in Harlem, in New York City, and this was the book *Stride Toward Freedom* that I wrote a few years ago. And she came in, I was writing and I heard someone say, 'Are you Reverend King?' and I didn't hardly look up, I just said yes, and by that time she leaned over and stabbed me and of course it was a near fatal stabbing. I was in the hospital for several weeks as a result of this.

FREEMAN But since the woman was demented, this was not strictly relevant to your campaign.

KING No, yet I don't think it can be totally divorced. Because if I hadn't been involved in this, she wouldn't have even known me.

FREEMAN Have you during this period, which must have been one of very great strain for you, have you felt frightened and even very lonely in your position of leadership?

KING Yes, I think honesty impels me to admit that there have been those times that I actually confronted fear. But I have always had something that gave me an inner sense of assurance, and an inner sense of security, in the final analysis. Even in the moments of loneliness, something ultimately came to remind me that in this struggle, because it is basically right, because it is a thrust forward to achieve something not just for Negro people, but something that will save the whole of mankind, and when I have come to see these things I always felt a sense of cosmic companionship. So that the loneliness and the fear have faded away because of a greater feeling of security, because of commitment to a moral ideal.

FREEMAN Does that carry you as far as feeling total confidence in yourself? For instance, for better or worse you've become the symbol now of Negro emancipation in the southern states. Now, are you an adequate symbol, do you feel that you are adequate?

KING Well, again I must confess that there are those moments when I feel a sense of inadequacy as a symbol. It is never easy for one to accept the role of symbolism, without going through constant moments of self-examination. And I must confess that there are moments when I begin to wonder whether I am adequate or whether I am able to face all of the challenges and even the responsibilities of this particular position.

FREEMAN Have you always found that you've been able to keep your wife and children with you or have you ever felt it necessary to send them away for safety?

KING There have been times that I have had to send them away for safety, particularly when we were in the state of Alabama. But my wife happens to be one of those very strong persons and one who is very concerned about this whole matter and very dedicated. And I can remember a moment when I sent her away for safety, I would look up a few days later and she was back home because she wanted to be there.

FREEMAN Dr King, clearly you're making progress in this. Now, could you make more progress if your demonstrations were based on more direct action, on strikes, for instance, in a more direct economic threat, in the way that some of the African people struggling for independence have tried to shape their destinies?

KING Well, I do feel that non-violent direct action is the most powerful approach in seeking to bring about racial justice. Now to a degree we have moved in this area. The Montgomery bus boycott was a limited move in this area, the sit-ins that have engulfed the whole South over the last few months, would be another move in this direction. This is non-violent direct action. Also the freedom rides. I think all of these things are certainly serving to speed up the process and I think the more we delve deeper into these particular areas, the more we will be able to bring about at least a speedy solution to the problem.

FREEMAN Some of your critics do say that you lack fire, that you're not really keen on challenging except on the margins of this problem. Now I expect that's unfair but I'd like to hear your answer to it.

KING Well, I don't know if I lack fire. I do feel that at times I am rather soft and maybe a little gentle but on the other hand I have strongly advocated direct action. I have made it clear that I believe that this is one of the most potent weapons available to oppressed people in their struggle for freedom. And human dignity. So that I don't consider this a marginal approach, I consider this as an approach going to the very depths. I have participated in sit-ins myself, I have been arrested as a result of my participating in sit-ins, with the students, at lunch counters, I served as one of the co-ordinators of the freedom rides, so that I don't think it is true to say that I am not in accord with these particular methods. I believe in them, and I have advocated them and participated in them.

FREEMAN I understand exactly why you believe in non-violence, but have you found it easy to persuade your followers that non-violence is really the best method? I mean, there must be a great temptation to take a poke back at a white man who hits you.

KING It is difficult at times, to convince people that this is the best way. And I guess it is difficult for all of us not to retaliate. But on the whole, I have been amazed at the tremendous response that we have gained when we have called for non-violent action. I look back over Montgomery and think of the fact that for all of these days, 381 days, more than 99.9 per cent of the Negro citizens participated in the boycott, they confronted harassing experiences, they confronted physical violence. And never did they retaliate with a single act of physical violence. And the same is true of the students' sit-in movement, which included thousands of students, and very few retaliated with physical violence. So that even though it is difficult, I think we have been able to get this method over in a most significant way.

FREEMAN Dr King, apart from the business of discrimination, are you a radical in other causes, do you follow the other great radical political causes in the world or not?

KING Well, I'm not sure what cause you mean –

FREEMAN Are you concerned, for instance, with, let's say, the abolishing of nuclear weapons?

KING Oh yes, I have worked very closely with this particular approach. I have worked with an organisation for sane nuclear policy in the United States, and I am a strong believer in disarmament and suspension of nuclear tests, and some methods being used to arouse the conscience of mankind on this most important issue. As I've said so often, I don't think the choice is any longer between violence and non-violence in a day when guided ballistic missiles are carving highways of death through the stratosphere, I think now it is a choice between non-violence and non-existence. So that I have strongly endorsed organisations that are fighting, are struggling in a creative, non-violent way, to arouse the conscience of mankind on this issue.

FREEMAN Well now, let me put to you a last question. You could live and work in many parts of the world where you'd be discriminated against much less than you were in the United States. You are, I suspect, a patriotic American citizen and you probably don't propose to live anywhere but the United States. Now, will you tell me why?

KING Well, I can only say that the United States is home for me, I was born there, and in spite of its shortcomings naturally there are things in the United States that I love and people that I love. I think we have a great tradition ideally, the democratic creed is a marvellous one, and my work is simply an attempt to say to America that you have a marvellous ideal and you should live up to it. And so when the students sat down at lunch counters and I decided to join with them I felt that we were in reality standing up for the best in the American dream. And certainly the best in the dream of all mankind for peace and brotherhood. So I live there with the feeling that we are moving in the right direction and with the feeling that this problem can be solved in the United States if enough people give themselves to it, if they devote their lives to breaking down all the barriers that separate men from men, on the basis of race or colour.

ALBERT FINNEY

INTRODUCTION

John Freeman's penultimate interview in March 1962 in what was by now his acclaimed series *Face to Face*, was with one of the few young people to appear on the programme. Albert Finney was then a bright-eyed, self-assured twenty-five-year-old brimming with talent, and already with an outstanding reputation for an actor still so young.

While still at drama school, he'd been described by critic Kenneth Tynan as 'a smouldering young Spencer Tracy': at Birmingham Rep Finney's Macbeth was seen by Charles Laughton who pronounced it bloody terrible. But it was at Stratford upon Avon when he stepped in to replace an injured Laurence Olivier in the title role of Coriolanus that he made his first big breakthrough – he was still only twenty-three.

His reputation grew swiftly. It was *Billy Liar* in 1960 that made his name more widely known, and then Arthur Seton in Karel Reitz's film, *Saturday Night and Sunday Morning*. A new wave of plays about the working class was spearheading a major renaissance in the theatre and spreading to British films. Finney's film role of Seton was as a lower-class, beer-swilling lout – a role that dismayed his mother, who worried that the public would identify Finney with the character. In fact he came from a respectable lower middle-class home in Salford – where his father was a bookmaker.

Shortly after, Finney played the title role in John Osborne's play *Luther*: a part that helped redress the balance. Since that time Finney's career has spanned theatre and cinema, directing and production. But perhaps, because he has never identified himself strongly with either of the two great companies, the National or the RSC, he has not consistently played the classic parts on which great theatre reputations are sustained.

But whatever role he plays, he leaves an impression of great power: the play *Orphans* in 1986 and films such as *Under The Volcano* and *The Dresser*. His is a commanding presence and here he is, over a quarter of a century ago, in his youthful prime.

INTERVIEW

FREEMAN Albert Finney, would you mind telling me first of all how old you are?

FINNEY Twenty-five.

FREEMAN And how old were you when you made your first professional appearance on the stage?

FINNEY Twenty . . . I was . . . was I? No, nineteen . . . almost twenty.

FREEMAN Almost twenty. . . . And how old were you when you played Coriolanus at Stratford and took over from Olivier, which is really when you first properly attracted national attention?

FINNEY What . . . nineteen, twenty, twenty-one . . . twenty-three I was.

FREEMAN So, at the age of twenty-five, in terms of box office you've become a great star, and the serious critics look upon you as one of the best prospects, let's say, since Olivier, or something like that – you've come an awful long way, by the time you're twenty-five. Now, it's widely believed, I think, among your public, that the character Arthur Seton in *Saturday Night and Sunday Morning*, which you played in the film, bears some close parallel to yourself and your own life – so let's just look at that for a minute. What sort of home do you come from?

FINNEY Well, I suppose really a lower middle-class home. . . . I had a marvellous childhood, I was always very happy . . . I remember it with great sort of joy.

FREEMAN Your father is, by profession – ?

FINNEY A bookmaker.

FREEMAN And therefore, I think it's probably safe to say he's never been really short of money?

FINNEY There is a slight false illusion about bookmakers, they're not all sort of tremendously wealthy and own great yachts, you know, which my father, in fact, doesn't do. But we were always comfortable.

FREEMAN A comfortable, solid, suburban end of Salford?

FINNEY Yes.

FREEMAN Now, what kind of schooling did you have?

FINNEY I went to Salford Grammar School . . . I entered at the sort
of high stream, on the high intelligence level, but I, for some reason,
I regarded the homework at the age of eleven rather as an imposition,
and in the first term I never did any. . . . So after one term in the
high stream I was put into the bottom stream, and there I remained
for about four years. . . . And I tried all the excuses of not doing
homework – now and again one thought one came up with an
original one, but of course the masters have had them all. And in the
fourth year for some reason I suddenly worked again, and I was put
up back in the high stream, and that burst of intellectual activity
lasted for two terms, then I faded rather, and didn't work very hard
after that.

FREEMAN Why did you try and get into the low stream – if you were
trying to, why . . . ?

FINNEY I didn't try to get into the lower stream, really . . . I mean, I
just sort of was put there because I didn't do my . . . I used to put ink
on my exercise books and say that I'd done my homework but it had
got covered up in ink, and that sort of thing – any excuse . . . I once
ran away from home – I don't know if my father knows this to this
day – because I hadn't done my maths homework, and I didn't want
to go in the next day and tell the teacher because I knew this was it,
and I got to the station and there was no train going where I wanted
to go – I was eleven – I was going to live on a mountain in Wales,
which the family called Fish Mountain, where we'd been for a
holiday, and I discovered that no trains went from Salford Station to
Prestatyn or Rhyl, so I went back home and climbed in again through
the lavatory window.

FREEMAN What did you like doing at that age?

FINNEY Well, I did a lot of sport at school . . . I used to play rugby
and cricket and tennis, and swim, and I liked climbing, and hiking.
. . . I did school plays, but didn't like doing homework – ever.

FREEMAN Before you ever thought of the possibility of going on the
stage, what were your ambitions for the future when you were grown
up?

FINNEY None really . . . there was nothing definitely planned in my
own head – there was no aim, no ambition.

FREEMAN What did your parents want you to do – anything?

FINNEY I don't know, we never sort of really discussed my future in such definite terms really.

FREEMAN Do you have now close relations with your parents?

FINNEY Well, yes . . . inasmuch as one can – I mean, I phone them, I see them, when I can. . . .

FREEMAN How many times have you seen them this year?

FINNEY Well, this year, once, they came down to London for two days. My father only can get away really when there's no racing, you know. . . . Lucky because there were quite a few days of snow and ice.

FREEMAN But you're an affectionate family?

FINNEY Oh yes, very close . . . very close.

FREEMAN Judging from the newspaper interviews, and what one can tell from the cuttings, your mother is a most remarkable woman. Is that true?

FINNEY Oh yes – marvellous . . . she's a great woman.

FREEMAN Do you ever consult your parents now about your professional career, or what you might do with your life?

FINNEY Not in any such terms, no . . . they're marvellous inasmuch as they've never interfered in a certain sense, you know, I suppose with being away from them, in reality, from the age of seventeen, they must have worried at that time, quite naturally, me being in London, but I think they think I've done all right. . . . I think in a certain sense they're quite willing to let me carry on.

FREEMAN If you had a crisis in your life, and a really difficult decision to take, would you go and talk to your parents about it, or not? Honestly.

FINNEY No, I don't think so, I think that I would try and manage it myself.

FREEMAN Does this mean that having come to London, and branched out into a very different sort of life, that to some extent at least you now reject their standards of taste or of behaviour?

FINNEY Well, in a certain way . . . when one is seventeen, and when one comes to London and becomes a student, one feels at first that you are different, that you're now, if you like, a Bohemian, that you're now living in a different world, and you're a very different person, that the old standards have gone . . . But in fact those seventeen years of one's upbringing are very in there, you know, and you cannot throw them out, even if you want to, and even now I react to certain things, rather surprisingly, in the way I was brought up to react. There are new influences in my life, new fields I've gone into . . . all quite naturally, so that to a certain extent I have moved away from my home and my upbringing, but at the same time there are still very strong sort of ties there, which I think are very useful for me, because in the theatre, in one's profession, there can be rather spoiling influences, and somehow the sort of – the sanity, or the . . . it's a marvellous anchor, I feel, for me.

FREEMAN When you go home now to your parents' house, does it still strike you as the most comfortable place in the world?

FINNEY Oh, it's marvellous – you can feel the nerves sort of resting, you know . . . you feel as if you can just sort of lie back. . . . It's not quite the same now because the telephone's going, and newspapers are saying: 'Oh, is Mr Finney there?'

FREEMAN What sort of life do you live now, in London? Is it true that you live in a suitcase?

FINNEY Not quite . . . a trunk and maybe three suitcases, now.

FREEMAN You have in fact got a permanent home now?

FINNEY Not quite a permanent home . . . I do live in a furnished flat, which isn't mine . . . but for the first time, in fact, I now want to have a flat of my own and put my own stuff in it . . . . But I've only recently started to get this feeling so I'm looking at the moment for a flat.

FREEMAN Yes. Well, all this of course is very conventional, solid, middle-class . . . very different from Arthur Seton, or even from Billy Liar, for that matter. Now, has it been a professional embarrassment to you being sort of type-cast at least in the public mind as a kind of North Midlands corner boy?

FINNEY Slightly, yes. . . . There's something in me which absolutely hates the sort of selling of an image to the public, you say that this is it, this is what it does, you know, that he sort of gets drunk all the time, and shoots guns at fat ladies all the time . . . you know, this I resent. And I was rather annoyed that when the film was shown, people saw me as Arthur Seton, I was also in *Billy Liar* and they would find no difference between the two characters, which to me are

absolutely different, you know . . . I do hate this feeling of that is
what you are . . . . One is an actor.

FREEMAN Well now, let's accept it that you're a very conventional
young actor of bourgeois tastes, and respectable dress . . . which part
that you've played, in fact, has given you the most satisfaction so far?

FINNEY I suppose this changes in a way, John, you know, because
now Luther gives me, or gave me, great satisfaction, but it depends on
the state one is in at the time . . . you know. . . . When I did
Coriolanus at Stratford, when I took over from Sir Laurence, I was in
a really bad state as regards acting, and somehow just having to go on
freed me, and it was marvellous to play Coriolanus and I enjoyed it
tremendously. But that was because the rest of the season, for me,
was rather black, you know, depends how one is, so I don't look back
on any particular part as a great high spot.

FREEMAN Do you have any ambition to play all through the classical
repertory, or do you now want to stick with contemporary plays?

FINNEY Oh no, I want to play all of those parts that are on the shelf,
you know . . . rather a considerable number of them.

FREEMAN Are you confident about playing the sort of romantic leads,
because those are the parts you haven't done very much so far?

FINNEY The romantic leads . . . for instance, Romeo?

FREEMAN Well, indeed, yes.

FINNEY I've never really wanted to play Romeo . . . I always feel, for
instance, that when he has to get out of the bedroom, the morning
when he's rushing off to Mantua, he should have taken Juliet with
him. . . . The end of the play is rather pointless, she should have gone
with him, I mean, they should have got in a boat and gone abroad.

FREEMAN I think you'd better not play Romeo . . .

FINNEY I'd better not play . . . Romeo.

FREEMAN Is there any particular living actor that you've taken as a
model or a master . . . even on points of technique? I'm not asking
you a sentimental question, but, I mean, have you watched Gielgud,
or Olivier, or whatever it may be, to see how they moved in
particular circumstances?

FINNEY When I'm in an audience and I'm watching an actor I can be
moved, but I'm also watching him . . . I can count while he does
something, to see how his technique is working, but that's his . . . I've
got to find out mine, the way I work . . . . This is where one needs

more practice when one acts. All the time one is finding out how your body works . . . you know. It's all right for him to do it that way, but you've got to find your way, and you can learn by watching other people act, but finally it's the amount of acting, or practice, if you like, that you do within your own body . . . I think.

FREEMAN Of course, your talents are very obvious, I mean we can see these, but you know the dark side of yourself which the rest of us don't see, now are there any particular technical difficulties in acting that you have to struggle to overcome? I mean, do you find it difficult to stand still, or to walk, or to laugh, or whatever it may be on the stage?

FINNEY One of them is my voice, inasmuch as the use of it . . . I, as an actor, tend to work emotionally. This is quite natural for a young actor, you know, because technique is lacking, natch . . . So, I work emotionally, on an emotional sort of surge, if you like, and what this can mean is that the vocal use of text suffers. Eventually with more experience one gets a balance between the text, the value of the text, and the emotional pump within you on stage. . . . At the moment I tend to sort of tear a bit at the text in order to get off this emotion, which I feel very strongly, and somehow I don't feel that I'm acting properly unless I'm going through marvellous feelings of sadness, joy, whatever . . . I think I have to learn to control this emotional drive, slightly, and to use what the author has set out for me to use. I tend perhaps to use his text as a vehicle for my emotional power. Not ignore completely his text, because I hope that I act his text, but I think I could perhaps use it more than I do.

FREEMAN Do you accept the description of yourself as being one of a new wave of actors? I mean, is this just a newspaper word or do you think there is a new wave of which you are a representative?

FINNEY Yes, I think there probably is, in a certain sense, because I think that public taste has changed somewhat . . . I mean, there are more plays written about more different subjects, but there are still a lot of plays on in London that could have been on perhaps twenty years ago.

FREEMAN Would you like to define to me any kind of common purpose, or common view of the world, that you and the group who come from the Midlands and the North Country have in common?

FINNEY Well, I don't know – in a certain sense this is a difficult thing to answer, John, because I am an interpreter . . . you know . . . I watch people and I watch myself. I often wondered why I am an actor, I think I am always watching and balancing, and sort of tabulating my own emotions and feelings in life, and the only way I can lose myself, and be self-conscious – I don't mean self-conscious, gauche, awkward, I mean self-conscious, aware – is when I'm acting . . . So I think this is why I'm an actor. So, consequently I don't think that I can really say, you know, what I want to show . . . I respond to text . . . I'm not an original artist, you know.

FREEMAN Quite, we draw conclusions about you and you offer the material. But what was it in fact that first made you want to be an actor? I mean, I don't want the story about how you left school, and so on, but there must have been something inside you.

FINNEY This is peculiar in a way, because I didn't ever feel that I wanted to be an actor. . . . The school I was at, the Salford Grammar School, the years I was there, did a tremendous number of plays . . . when I was in those plays I thought it would be quite nice to be an actor, but no more than when I played rugby for the school, or cricket, or whatever, I thought it would be quite good to be a rugby player, or a cricketer . . . . Then eventually the headmaster suggested that I went to drama school . . . I said yes, mainly because I thought it would be marvellous to be in London, you know, as a student, because I'd read about them painting statues white, and running about the streets, and all that stuff, that would be marvellous. So I thought, Yes we'll go to London, but after being at RADA for two terms I realised what I was doing, and I also realised that I enjoyed it, and this supposedly was going to be my career, and I sort of buckled down to it, and got working at it.

FREEMAN And since then you really have got satisfaction out of it?

FINNEY Yes absolutely.

FREEMAN You always talk about working – at least your press cuttings suggest that you go to work each evening, you work on the stage – now, do you regard your job as done when the curtain comes down, or do you subscribe at all to the old-fashioned view that the actor is, to some extent, a servant of the public in his private life, as well?

FINNEY Not at all. I think the actor only owes the audience good work in the theatre . . . I don't feel that an actor's private life has got anything to do with them whatsoever.

FREEMAN Well, do you think that's completely consistent with the business that you have to go into, whether you like it or not, to some extent, of selling your personality: that on the one hand you enjoy the limelight on the stage, on the other hand you fade out of it as fast as you possibly can as soon as you're off the stage – is there a temperamental inconsistency here, or not?

FINNEY No, I don't think so, because I am an actor . . . I mean, you know, that one works in a theatre, or in a studio in front of a camera.

FREEMAN Yes, but you depend also on audiences a bit, isn't there a danger that you may cut yourself off too much from, well, the fertilising element, if you like, in your work?

FINNEY No, because I think that if one can retain a certain sense of freedom. . . . When you become successful or whatever, you get a bit of money, you know, you go round in a large car and you can live very expensively, and then eventually all the people you see are very servile waiters and very expensively dressed diners, you never see sort of people . . . . Now, I'm acting people, it's my job, my life, if you like, and I've got to see them, so in a certain sense if people get in their head that when I leave the theatre I just want to go out into the night, and be alone, then I surely am able to watch people, feel that I can. This is very important to me.

FREEMAN Do you in fact go round in a large car?

FINNEY No, I have a Mini-Minor . . . not a large car.

FREEMAN So, in fact, although obviously, in one sense nowadays, you're in the money, you still lead a pretty modest life?

FINNEY I think so, yes.

FREEMAN What do you spend money on? Extravagantly . . . Clothes? Horses? Women?

FINNEY Women, not tremendously, no. . . . Horses, I don't bet. . . .

FREEMAN No, I meant the riding.

FINNEY A bit of riding yes, I spend it on that. I also spend money on odd lessons in the guitar and things like that, and voice lessons, but I don't spend tremendously.

FREEMAN On the whole you're not really an extravagant person?

FINNEY I don't think so.

FREEMAN How do you treat your fans? Do you reply to their letters?

FINNEY Yes . . . I didn't at first, I felt this was a great sort of intrusion. But in fact I thought I should and I do. I don't have any photographs, I don't send photographs because I don't have any.

FREEMAN Do you meet them when they stand at the stage door at the end of the show?

FINNEY Yes.

FREEMAN Now, you've often gone on record about not liking long runs, but, all right, oughtn't a disciplined professional to be able to run at least for a year without –

FINNEY Yes, but I think it's bad for an actor, because in a way if you're playing, for instance, in *Billy Liar* . . . after I'd played Billy Liar for three months, after a while you get sort of part drunk, that although you're doing it each evening, and it's going through your head, you've done it so often you can't think it properly, and also one gets frustrated by acting that physical shape . . . because in that I tried to make myself look more awkward, physically gaucher, thinner, smaller, weaker, and all that, and some nights, you know, one wants to come on and expand, one wants to come on and be romantic, or be strong or whatever, and playing the same part eight times a week, year in, you can't see the end of it, it's sort of limitless, you know, stretching on for ever . . . . You don't know when you're going to get out of it, or when it's going to end, because it's a success, which you're grateful for, but I think it's terribly important for a young actor to play as many parts as possible. This is why there should be more repertoire theatres in London, where an actor could, you know, some nights come on stage two nights a week play somebody weak and small, two nights a week play somebody big and strong, you know, vary himself, stretch himself, lose himself.

FREEMAN This I can understand, but looking at yourself in a very self-critical way now, do you think this is a defect of either temperament or technique on your part, that you'd be a more complete actor if you were prepared to face the long run with more equanimity?

FINNEY No.

FREEMAN Has it ever struck you that you're perhaps too young to enjoy stardom yet to the full – do you enjoy it, or would you have liked to go a bit more slowly?

FINNEY I don't know . . . in a way . . . perhaps qualify stardom, John.

FREEMAN Well, the responsibilities of being answerable to such a big public as you are now.

FINNEY I don't feel that so much . . . I mean, one does feel pressures obviously, pressures of having to sort of maintain a standard, quite naturally, and sometimes one feels it would be better to stay away, it

183

would be marvellous perhaps to go into a quiet theatre in the provinces somewhere and work quietly . . . . Often I do think perhaps I did come to London too soon, and that I should have waited till I was more formed as an actor, because I'm still learning a lot, and I sometimes feel perhaps I've got so much to learn in such a sort of exposed position, you know.

FREEMAN What about the more personal problems of an actor – I mean marriage and personal friendships, and so on? Now, your own marriage, as we know, broke up, but was that due to the inevitable strains of the stage, or do you think it was your fault?

FINNEY Well, I think it was my fault . . . when I got married there was nothing more I wanted to do than get married, and I was terribly in love . . . . But I was too young, really, and also the marriage in fact broke up when my acting was going through a very bad phase. It's too close, somehow, to analyse that.

FREEMAN Do you look at this as being a mistake on your part?

FINNEY No . . . I don't feel anything's a mistake, John, if you come through the other side of it . . . and you know about it. You conceive, or start to feel why – I don't think it's a mistake.

FREEMAN Would you be prepared to face marriage again?

FINNEY I suppose so, yes . . . yes.

FREEMAN Do you fall in love easily?

FINNEY No, not in love. . . . Well, I don't know, I've been in love now, I think, about four times . . . the first time was when I was fifteen, but four times in ten years – is that too much? I don't know, it's been rather good . . . .

FREEMAN Leaving marriage on one side, do you have a lot of close friends?

FINNEY No . . . I don't go into close friendships very easily, somehow. I've always found it rather difficult to make close friends of actors. . . . I have a lot of good friends, but not very many close friends.

FREEMAN But what about your private life that you keep so very private; now, is this still with stage people, or do you mix with different people?

FINNEY Well, stage people really . . .

FREEMAN Mostly with stage people . . . . Would you say you're a lonely person?

FINNEY Sometimes I do feel lonely, but I think a certain amount of loneliness is inevitable for a person who is like myself, who watches things very carefully, who observes things . . . somehow . . . I think so.

FREEMAN Do you even think perhaps that it's necessary for the artist to have a certain amount of loneliness, while he finds his feet?

FINNEY In his own head there's a loneliness, in one's own head, you know, you're not lonely for people or for company, but there's a loneliness because of what is life, of one's thoughts . . . . What I want to do in the theatre, or what one feels one wants to act, one can only communicate it really by doing it, by acting it. So in one's own head these feelings, these feelings of creation, if you like, are floating about, and you can't put them to work in company, so therefore there is a loneliness, because there's something in one's head one can't share in company, in a room, or with people, one only can do it perhaps one day in the future, through one's work . . . .

FREEMAN Yes. Do you feel that the intense professional life you've lived for the last two years, and your early success, on the whole has helped you to grow up and to achieve adult attitudes, or has it tended to hold you back, by making you concentrate on the unreal things of life?

FINNEY I think anyway I'm a slow maturer, as they say . . . I mean, I think in a certain sense this is why as a schoolboy I never had any sort of definite, you know, feelings of what I wanted to do, and only now, very recently, am I . . . . I am in a way slightly still going through a sort of identity complex because of moving from a certain kind of environment when I was seventeen, and all these things, you know, the new influences, the new changes, so I still don't quite know what I am, in a sense . . . . But perhaps an actor never does know what he is, because he's always very different.

FREEMAN Well now, I want to ask you, as a last question, something which goes right in there. Look at yourself, very honestly, and very self-critically, and tell me what, in your own estimate, is your greatest personal weakness?

FINNEY Self-indulgence, I think.

ACKNOWLEDGEMENTS

The publisher wishes to thank the following for their permission to reproduce copyright material:

Joan Bakewell; Lord Birkett; Professor Anthony Clare; Joan Daves (interview with Martin Luther King); Adam Faith; Christopher Farley (interview with Bertrand Russell); J. G. Ferguson Publishing Company (interview with Carl Gustav Jung); Albert Finney; The Rt. Hon. John Freeman; Livia Gollancz; The Henry Moore Foundation; Stirling Moss; The Hon. Christopher Reith; Francis Sitwell; Roger Storey (interview with Gilbert Harding); and Auberon Waugh.

Acknowledgement and thanks are also due to Frances Walker, who helped to research Joan Bakewell's introductions to the recent series.

All the photographs are BBC copyright except: Camera Press pages 34 (photo Tom Blau), 71 (photo Terence Spencer), 81 and 110.